EDAMAME
(e h • d a h • MAH • meh)

60 Tempting Recipes Featuring America's Hottest New Vegetable

EDAMAME
(e h • d a h • M A H • m e h)

Anne Egan

RODALE

Printed in the United States of America
Rodale Inc. makes every effort to use acid-free ∞, recycled paper ♻.

Photographs by Mitch Mandel

Book design by Christina Gaugler

Front cover recipe: Salted Edamame (page 12)

Library of Congress Cataloging-in-Publication Data

Egan, Anne.
   Edamame : 60 tempting recipes featuring America's hottest new vegetable / Anne Egan.
      p.   cm.
   Includes index.
    ISBN 1–57954–723–0   hardcover
    1. Cookery (Soybeans)   I. Title.
  TX803.S6E32   2003
  641.6'5655—dc21   2003005643

Distributed to the book trade by St. Martin's Press

2 4 6 8 10 9 7 5 3 1   hardcover

RODALE
WE INSPIRE AND ENABLE PEOPLE TO IMPROVE
THEIR LIVES AND THE WORLD AROUND THEM

FOR MORE OF OUR PRODUCTS
WWW.RODALESTORE.COM
(800) 848-4735

For Isabella

Contents

ACKNOWLEDGMENTS

Many thanks to all who contributed to this book, especially Kathy Baruffi, JoAnn Brader, Kathy Dvorsky, Christina Gaugler, Mitch Mandel, Paul Piccuito, Kimberly Tweed, and Marianne Zanzarella.

Introduction

Sweet, nutty-flavored edamame, green vegetable soybeans harvested just before maturity, are a welcome surprise for anyone who wants to add a healthy and exciting new ingredient to meals. Similar in flavor to sweet peas and lima beans, edamame are so delicious that most people can't believe they're actually eating soy. Readily available in most markets, both fresh in the summer and frozen year-round, edamame are still new to most cooks' repertoires. From appetizers to main and side dishes, the following recipes will show you how to incorporate edamame into every meal.

1

NAME GAME

These earthy beans are bursting with bountiful nutrients, including a whopping 11 grams of high-quality protein per half-cup. No wonder the Chinese once called them "meat without the bones." The Japanese originated the name, calling them edamame, which means "beans on a branch." The small, oval-shaped beans are also known by a variety of other names, including green vegetable soybeans, edible green soybeans, soybeans in the pod, branch beans, immature soybeans, sweet beans, and beer beans.

HISTORY

Soybeans are a food as rich in history as they are in flavor. As people have migrated all over the world, they have transported this ancient food staple with them. The journey began in China more than 4,000 years ago, where wild soybeans were plentiful. Regarded as one of the five principal and sacred crops, they were used medicinally as well as for food.

As time passed, soybeans, with more than 20,000 varieties, became the most widely used food plant in the world. Buddhist priests, eager to expand their vegetarian diets, embraced soybeans, taking them, along with the good word, on their journeys. Other travelers, including soldiers and merchants, continued to spread the news about these wholesome legumes.

However, when Portuguese traders and other Europeans brought soybeans back to their countries, people were reluctant to try them—they just didn't seem to fit into traditional cuisines. The reception was just as cool in the United States, despite several attempts to win converts.

In America and Europe, soybeans were like an extra on a stage set—they only got a chance as a stand-in. During the Civil War, soldiers used them as a substitute for coffee beans. Later, the boll weevil, which wiped out many cotton crops, provided a roundabout opportunity to grow soybeans in the 1920s. The plants flourished on the barren cotton fields, and much of the equipment used for cotton worked for harvesting soybeans. The reputation of these hearty beans then spread to the Midwest, where most of them became inexpensive animal feed until a new demand for soybean oil developed.

Soybean oil has been useful in many industrial products, including everything from linoleum to soap. Henry Ford often adapted soybean oil for use in plastics, and it was rumored that each of his vehicles contained at least a bushel of the versatile beans. Even today, many manufactured items, possibly even the ink on this page, are made from soybeans. Many began relying on their nutrition to take the place of meats and other animal products.

In the '60s, with the counterculture trend toward vegetarianism, soybeans rolled back into fashion as a food; they were touted as a nutrition powerhouse and a thrifty main course. However, this interest never really became mainstream. Although known as a terrific source of protein, soybeans in all their varieties continued to have an image problem in the United States until recent studies showed the health benefits associated with soy foods.

Recently the sushi craze has introduced edamame to many consumers. Japanese restaurant owners became pioneers, expanding the audience for soybeans by offering edamame to their customers as an appetizer. Many restaurants and bars replaced boring pretzels or peanuts with these fun salty pods.

THE HOTTEST HEALTH FOOD TODAY

The increasing popularity of vegetarianism among young people and the boomers' quest for a better quality of life as they age are just two forces that are quickly making edamame a favorite way to enjoy the many health benefits of soybeans. And you don't have to pretend you're eating something else, as with traditional soy products like tofu and tempeh.

As a complete protein, soybeans contain all the essential amino acids, including eight not produced by the body. Animal-based foods are the only other source of complete protein, but they usually contain saturated fat. Edamame and other varieties of soybeans, on the other hand, are low in saturated fat and have no cholesterol.

A good source of fiber, they also contain omega-3s, the essential fatty acids that maintain heart health by deterring the formation of blood clots. Omega-3s are the good fats that promote optimum heart and brain function, and we can only get them from food because the body cannot produce them. Edamame are also high in vitamin A, B-complex vitamins, calcium, and iron.

An antioxidant powerhouse, edamame are rich in beta-carotene and contain isoflavones, plant-based estrogens. Found predominantly in plants from the pea family, such as soybeans, isoflavones are often credited with helping to fight heart disease and prevent cancer. In fact, the Food and Drug Administration has recognized that consuming 25 milligrams of isoflavones daily can be beneficial in lowering heart-disease risk. One half-cup of edamame provides approximately 35 milligrams of isoflavones, 126 calories, 11 grams of protein, 10 grams of carbs, 4 grams of dietary fiber, and just 6 grams of fat.

Fortunately for the health-conscious consumers of today, edamame entered the picture just when they were most necessary. With a taste and appearance that are more appealing, edamame have a distinct advantage over many other soy foods. As more people learn that what they eat can affect everything from their mood to their chances of developing cancer, they are pleased to discover that these sweet and beneficial vegetable soybeans are easily adapted into their daily diets.

SELECTION

Most of the commercially available edamame in the United States are sold frozen, either shelled or unshelled. The unshelled are ideal for snacking—kids of all ages enjoy popping the cooked beans out of the shell as they do with peanuts. However, the shelled edamame are preferable for everything else because they are ready to use in any recipe.

Fresh edamame are available in the summer months. Look for bright green pods with plump beans. Your best chance to find them will be at farmers' markets or supermarkets that offer local, seasonal produce. You'll see them still on the branch in large bunches or removed from the branch and sold loose in pods.

PREPARATION

Edamame often have a fuzzy shell. When you cook fresh edamame to be eaten out of the hand, there's an easy way to remove the fuzz if you'd like. Rub the pods between your hands along with some kosher salt. Rinse the beans in cold water before cooking. If you will be shelling the pods, this step is unnecessary.

To cook in the pod, steam the edamame pods for 5 to 10 minutes until bright green and tender.

Shelled beans will be called for more often in these recipes. Whether you use fresh or frozen, the amount of cooking time will depend on the recipe. Beans that will be part of a crunchy salad only need to be boiled in salted water for 5 minutes. If you'll be making a dip, however, you'll want the beans to cook longer so they will be very tender. This should take about 10 to 15 minutes. Each recipe gives a suggested cooking time. You may also remove one bean from the pot and test its doneness. Typically, edamame are served when they are tender-crisp.

If you grow your own or have access to a farmer who does, you may want to purchase enough to freeze for later in the year. Blanch the pods by plunging them into salted water for 5 minutes and then into an ice bath. Spread the pods on a layer of paper towels and dry before placing in zip-top bags to freeze. If this is too much work for you, fear not—there are many brands of frozen edamame available in supermarkets.

GROW YOUR OWN

Edamame seeds are readily available, and home gardeners can now find varieties suitable for planting in different climate zones.

Jeff Moyer has been growing edamame for more than 10 years at the Rodale Institute in Kutztown, Pennsylvania, an education, training, and research farm facility dedicated to promoting healthy food grown in healthy soil. "They're easy to grow. You treat them just like peas, only you don't have to trellis them," says Moyer. The handsome plants grow on bushes and are self-supporting.

Moyer plants his rows wide, about 30 inches apart. Within the rows, the seeds can be close, 1 to 2 inches apart. They're daylight sensitive, but shorter-season varieties are available for northern states. Moyer describes soybeans as "plastic," meaning that they're fairly adaptive even if there is some variation in daylight.

Like most leguminous plants, they can take nitrogen from the air and put it into the soil. This feature of their unique root structure, which has thousands of tiny nodules, means that they don't need nitrogen fertilizer. In fact, soybeans are so good for the soil, some farmers grow them just for fertilizer. Soybeans also tolerate summer heat and cool summer nights well.

Sow edamame several times during the summer to allow for a staggered harvest, with a crop in late summer and early autumn.

It's also important to harvest them at the right time. If they're picked too soon, they'll be tiny, and if they're picked late, they'll dry out. Color and plumpness of the bean are both clues for readiness. The pods should still be bright green, similar in color to a snow pea, and the beans should almost fill the pod. If they've gone yellow, it's too late.

There's a limited shelf life for fresh edamame, so if you get a bumper crop, follow the directions on page 6 for freezing.

"The flavor is very pleasing. I don't know anyone who has eaten them and not liked them," says Moyer, who is farm manager at the institute. "When we first started growing them, we'd take a few boxes to the local grocery store to see how folks reacted to them. Well, we couldn't supply them fast enough. Everybody loved them so much!"

Here are a few sources for edamame seeds.

Bountiful Gardens
18001 Shafer Ranch Road
Willits, CA 95490
(707) 459-6410
www.bountifulgardens.org
Specializes in heirloom-quality organic seeds

Evergreen Seeds
PO Box 17538
Anaheim, CA 92817
(714) 637-5769
www.evergreenseeds.com
Specializes in Asian vegetables

Fedco Seeds
PO Box 520-A
Waterville, ME 04903
www.fedcoseeds.com
A cooperative seed company

Johnny's Selected Seeds
184 Foss Hill Road
Albion, ME 04910
(207) 861-3901
www.johnnyseeds.com

APPETIZERS

From simple to sophisticated,
edamame add flavor and fun to
these first-course bites

11

SALTED EDAMAME

1 pound fresh or frozen unshelled edamame

½ teaspoon coarse salt

🌿 Place a large bowl of ice water on the counter.

🌿 Bring a large pot of water to a boil over high heat. Add the edamame
and cook until bright green and tender, 10 minutes for fresh, 5 minutes
for frozen. Remove the edamame from the boiling water with a slotted
spoon and place in the ice water. Drain well.

🌿 Place the edamame in a serving bowl and toss with the salt. To eat, pop
open the shells and slip the edamame into your mouth. Serve with a
bowl for empty shells.

Makes 8 servings

ROASTED EDAMAME

Prep time: 3 minutes • Cook time: 13 minutes

PHOTOGRAPH ON PAGE 57

1 tablespoon extra-virgin olive oil

½ teaspoon wasabi powder

½ teaspoon dried basil, crushed

½ teaspoon salt

¼ teaspoon freshly ground black pepper

⅛ teaspoon ground ginger

2 cups shelled edamame

Preheat the oven to 375°F. Lightly coat a large baking sheet with olive oil cooking spray.

In a large bowl, whisk together the oil, wasabi powder, basil, salt, pepper, and ginger. Add the edamame and toss to coat well. Place on the prepared baking sheet and bake for 13 minutes, stirring once, until lightly browned. Place on a rack to cool.

Makes 8 servings

EDAMAME SALSA

1½ cups shelled edamame

4 tablespoons fresh lime juice

2 tablespoons extra-virgin olive oil

1 teaspoon salt

1 teaspoon grated lime peel

1 can (11 ounces) whole-kernel corn, drained

1 small tomato, chopped

1 jalapeño pepper, seeded and minced (wear plastic gloves when handling)

½ small red onion, chopped

1 tablespoon finely chopped fresh cilantro

🌿 In a medium saucepan, bring 3 cups salted water to a boil over high heat. Add the edamame and return to a boil. Cook the edamame for 5–7 minutes, or until tender-crisp. Drain the edamame and rinse under cold running water. Drain well.

🌿 Meanwhile, in a large serving bowl, whisk together the lime juice, oil, salt, and lime peel. Add the edamame, corn, tomato, pepper, onion, and cilantro to the bowl and toss to coat well.

Makes 8 servings

ZESTY GARLIC DIP

Prep time: 15 minutes • Cook time: 1 hour

1 large bulb garlic (2¾ ounces)

3 cups chicken broth

3 cups shelled edamame

2 tablespoons extra-virgin olive oil

1 tablespoon chopped fresh rosemary

2 teaspoons fresh lemon juice

¼ teaspoon salt

Preheat the oven to 350°F. Place the garlic in the center of a piece of foil. Seal the foil around the garlic and bake for 50–60 minutes, or until very tender. Remove the garlic from the foil and cool.

Meanwhile, in a medium saucepan, bring the broth to a boil over high heat. Add the edamame and return to a boil. Cook the edamame for 25 minutes, or until tender. Drain the edamame, reserving ½ cup of the broth.

Place 1 cup of the edamame in a blender or food processor with the reserved broth, oil, rosemary, lemon juice, and salt. Peel the roasted garlic cloves and squeeze each clove to extract the garlic. Add the garlic to the blender or food processor. Blend or process the mixture until smooth. Spoon the puree into a bowl. Stir in the remaining edamame.

Makes 8 servings

GUACAMOLE

Guacamole

- 1½ cups shelled edamame
- 1 avocado, pitted and peeled
- ¼ cup sour cream
- 3 scallions, chopped
- 2 plum tomatoes, chopped
- 2 cloves garlic, minced
- 2 tablespoons fresh lemon juice
- 1 teaspoon salt
- ¼ teaspoon hot-pepper sauce

Chips

- 2 tablespoons extra-virgin olive oil
- 1½ teaspoons ground cumin
- 4 flour tortillas (7"–8" each)
- ½ teaspoon coarse salt

🌿 Preheat the oven to 350°F.

🌿 *To make the guacamole:* In a medium saucepan, bring 3 cups salted water to a boil over high heat. Add the edamame and return to a boil. Cook the edamame for 10 minutes. Drain well.

🌿 Place the edamame in a bowl and mash with a potato masher. Add the avocado and mash. Stir in the sour cream, scallions, tomatoes, garlic, lemon juice, salt, and hot-pepper sauce.

🌿 *To make the chips:* Coat a baking sheet with cooking spray. In a small bowl, combine the oil and cumin. With a pastry brush, brush 1 side of each tortilla with the oil mixture. Sprinkle each tortilla with some salt. Cut each tortilla into 8 wedges.

🌿 Arrange the wedges on the prepared baking sheet. Bake for 7–8 minutes, or until the tortillas are light brown. Serve the guacamole with the tortilla chips.

Makes 8 servings

CHICKEN QUESADILLAS

Prep time: 30 minutes • Cook time: 40 minutes

1 cup shelled edamame

1 medium poblano chile pepper (4 ounces),
halved (wear plastic gloves when handling)

2 tablespoons vegetable oil

1 tablespoon chili powder

1 small yellow squash, halved lengthwise and
sliced

1 large tomato, chopped

1¼ teaspoons salt

4 ounces cooked chicken, chopped (1 cup)

1 baking potato, peeled and thinly sliced

1 tablespoon butter, melted

1 cup shredded Monterey Jack cheese

Sour cream (for garnish)

Preheat the broiler. In a medium saucepan, bring 2 cups salted water to a boil over high heat. Add the edamame and return to a boil. Cook the edamame for 5–7 minutes, or until tender-crisp. Drain well.

Meanwhile, arrange the pepper halves on the rack in a broiler pan. Broil the pepper halves 4" from the heat for 5–8 minutes, or until the skin has blackened. Place the pepper halves in a brown paper bag and seal. When the pepper halves are cool enough to handle, remove and discard the skin. Chop the pepper.

Heat 1 tablespoon of the oil in a large skillet over medium heat. Add the chili powder and cook for 1 minute, until fragrant.

Add the squash and cook, stirring often, for 2 minutes.

Increase the heat to medium-high. Add the edamame, pepper, tomato, and 1 teaspoon of the salt and cook, stirring often, for 3 minutes.

🌿 Add the chicken and heat through.

🌿 Preheat the oven to 450°F. Place the potato slices in a bowl with the re-maining tablespoon of oil, butter, and remaining ¼ teaspoon salt. Toss the potatoes to coat.

🌿 Coat two 8" ovenproof nonstick skillets with cooking spray. Arrange one-quarter of the potatoes, overlapping slightly, to cover the bottom of each skillet. Heat the skillets over medium heat and cook, for 8–10 minutes, or until the edges of the potato slices begin to brown and the potatoes stick together.

🌿 Spoon half of the edamame mixture over the potatoes in each skillet. Sprinkle half of the cheese over the edamame mixture in each skillet.

🌿 Arrange one-quarter of the potatoes, overlapping slightly, to cover the filling in each skillet. Place the skillets in the oven and bake for 10 minutes.

🌿 Gently run a spatula around the edge of each potato quesadilla to loosen. Place a plate over the skillet and carefully turn the potato que-sadilla onto the plate. Gently slide the potato quesadilla back into the skillet. Repeat with the remaining potato quesadilla.

🌿 Place the skillets over medium heat. Cook for 5 minutes, or until the bottom layer of the potatoes is browned and tender.

🌿 To serve, cut each quesadilla into quarters. Place 2 pieces on each of 4 plates. Garnish with a dollop of sour cream.

Makes 4 servings

SHRIMP TOSTADAS

1 cup shelled edamame

2 tablespoons extra-virgin olive oil

1 large clove garlic, sliced

1 small red onion, cut into thin wedges

1 serrano chile pepper, minced (wear plastic gloves when handling)

1 teaspoon ground cumin

½ pound medium shrimp, peeled, deveined, and cut lengthwise in half

1 teaspoon salt

1 cup grape tomatoes, halved

2 ounces shredded Monterey Jack cheese

6 whole wheat flour tortillas (8" each)

6 chives (optional)

🌿 In a medium saucepan, bring 2 cups salted water to a boil over high heat. Add the edamame and return to a boil. Cook the edamame for 5–7 minutes, or until tender-crisp. Drain well.

🌿 Heat the oil in a large skillet over medium heat. Add the garlic and cook for 1 minute, or until fragrant.

🌿 Add the onion, chile, and cumin and cook, stirring occasionally, for 2 minutes. Increase the heat to medium-high. Add the edamame, shrimp, and salt and cook, stirring often, for 1 minute.

🌿 Add the tomatoes and cook, stirring often, for 3 minutes, or until the shrimp are opaque and the tomatoes have softened. Spoon the shrimp mixture into a bowl and cool slightly. Stir in the cheese.

🌿 To serve, spoon about ½ cup of the shrimp mixture onto each tortilla. Roll up each tortilla and if you like, tie it in the center with a chive.

Makes 6 servings

SAVORY MUSHROOM TART

Prep time: 30 minutes • Cook time: 30 minutes
PHOTOGRAPH ON PAGE 55

½ package (17.3 ounces) frozen puff pastry sheets, thawed

1 egg, beaten

1 cup shelled edamame

2 tablespoons extra-virgin olive oil

2 large shallots, cut into thin wedges

4 ounces shiitake mushrooms, trimmed and sliced

4 ounces cremini and/or oyster mushrooms, trimmed and sliced

¾ teaspoon salt

¼ teaspoon freshly ground black pepper

2 teaspoons minced fresh thyme

2 tablespoons Madeira wine

4 ounces goat cheese, crumbled

🌿 Preheat the oven to 400°F. Coat a large baking sheet with cooking spray.

🌿 On a lightly floured surface with a floured rolling pin, roll the puff pastry into a 13" square. Using a sharp knife, cut a 1" frame from the pastry square. (The pastry square will now measure 11".) Brush the edge of the pastry square with some of the egg. Holding opposite corners of the pastry frame in each hand, bring the corners up criss-crossing over the pastry square (passing one corner over the other). Press the pastry frame down onto the edges of the pastry square. (The corners are now opposite their original position and there is a twist in the pastry frame in the remaining opposing corners.) Place the pastry on the prepared baking sheet.

🌿 Bake the pastry for 8 minutes, or until lightly browned.

🌿 Meanwhile, in a medium saucepan, bring 2 cups salted water to a boil over high heat. Add the edamame and return to a boil. Cook the edamame for 5–7 minutes, or until tender-crisp. Drain well.

🌿 Heat the oil in a large skillet over medium heat. Add the shallots and cook, stirring often, for 5 minutes.

🌿 Add the mushrooms, salt, and pepper and cook, stirring often, for 5 minutes.

🌿 Add the edamame, thyme, and wine and cook, stirring often, for 2 minutes, or until the mushrooms are tender. Stir in the cheese.

🌿 Spoon the edamame mixture onto the bottom of the pastry tart. Brush the border with some of the remaining egg.

🌿 Bake the tart for 8–10 minutes, or until the pastry is golden brown and the filling is heated through. Cut into 12 pieces.

Makes 12 servings

SIMPLE BRUSCHETTA

Prep time: 15 minutes • Cook time: 10 minutes
PHOTOGRAPH ON PAGE 57

 1 cup shelled edamame

¼ cup drained oil-packed sun-dried tomatoes, finely chopped

¼ cup fresh basil, chopped

 2 tablespoons grated Parmesan cheese

 1 tablespoon extra-virgin olive oil

 1 tablespoon drained nonpareil capers

16 diagonal slices French baguette, each ½" thick

 1 large clove garlic, halved crosswise

 1 plum tomato, halved crosswise

🌿 Preheat the broiler. In a medium saucepan, bring 2 cups salted water to a boil over high heat. Add the edamame and return to a boil. Cook the edamame for 5–7 minutes, or until tender-crisp. Drain well.

🌿 Place the edamame in a bowl with the sun-dried tomatoes, basil, cheese, oil, and capers, tossing to combine.

🌿 Arrange the bread on a rack in a broiler pan. Or place the bread on a grill over medium coals. Broil or grill the bread for 3–4 minutes, or until toasted, turning once.

🌿 Rub the cut side of the garlic and the cut side of the plum tomato on one side of each slice of bread.

🌿 Spoon about 1 tablespoon of the edamame mixture on each slice of bread.

Makes 8 servings

CURRIED CROQUETTES

Prep time: 45 minutes • Cook time: 10 minutes
PHOTOGRAPH ON PAGE 56

1½ cups shelled edamame

1 large baking potato (10 ounces), peeled and cut into 1" pieces

2 tablespoons + ¼ cup vegetable oil

1 medium onion, chopped

1 tablespoon curry powder

2 teaspoons fresh lemon juice

¾ teaspoon salt

¼ cup fresh cilantro, chopped

1 egg beaten with 1 tablespoon water

3 tablespoons all-purpose flour

¼ cup plain dried bread crumbs

1 container (8 ounces) plain yogurt

2 tablespoons finely chopped fresh mint

1 teaspoon grated lemon peel

In a medium saucepan, bring 3 cups salted water to a boil over high heat. Add the edamame and return to a boil. Cook the edamame for 10 minutes. Drain well.

Meanwhile, place the potato in a medium saucepan with enough salted water to cover. Bring to a boil over high heat. Cook for 15 minutes, or until very tender. Drain well.

Heat 2 tablespoons of the oil in a 10" skillet over medium heat. Add the onion and cook, stirring often, for 5 minutes.

Add the curry powder and cook, stirring often, for 1 minute.

Add the edamame, potato, lemon juice, and ½ teaspoon of the salt, stirring to coat. Using a potato masher, coarsely mash the edamame mixture. Stir in the cilantro. Shape 2 tablespoons of the edamame mixture into a 2" round disk. Repeat with the remaining edamame mixture.

Dip each disk into the beaten egg, the flour, and then the bread crumbs. Place the croquettes on a wire rack for 20 minutes to dry.

Heat the remaining ¼ cup oil in a large skillet over medium heat. Cook the croquettes in batches, turning once, for 4 minutes, or until golden brown.

In a small bowl, combine the yogurt, mint, lemon peel, and remaining ¼ teaspoon salt. Serve the yogurt sauce with the croquettes.

Makes 8 servings

VEGETABLE NAPOLEONS

Prep time: 50 minutes • Cook time: 1 hour and 20 minutes

   2 cups chicken broth

1¼ teaspoons salt

   1 cup yellow cornmeal

   ½ cup + 2 tablespoons grated Parmesan cheese

   ½ teaspoon freshly ground black pepper

1½ cups shelled edamame

   2 tablespoons extra-virgin olive oil

   3 large cloves garlic, sliced

   1 bulb fennel (1 pound), trimmed, cored, and chopped

   3 cups arugula or baby spinach

   2 cups cherry tomatoes, quartered

   3 ounces shredded smoked mozzarella (¾ cup)

🌿 Line a 13" × 9" baking pan with foil and coat it with cooking spray.

🌿 In a large saucepan, bring 2 cups water, the broth, and ½ teaspoon of the salt to a boil over high heat. Gradually add the cornmeal in a slow steady stream, stirring constantly to avoid lumps. Reduce the heat to medium and cook, stirring constantly, for 40 minutes, or until the polenta pulls away from the side of the saucepan and no longer tastes raw. Remove the saucepan from the heat and stir in ½ cup of the Parmesan and ¼ teaspoon of the pepper. Pour the polenta into the prepared pan. Using a wet spatula, spread the polenta into an even thickness. Cover and set aside until set.

🌿 In a medium saucepan, bring 3 cups salted water to a boil. Add the edamame and return to a boil. Cook the edamame for 5–7 minutes, or until tender-crisp. Drain well.

✍ Heat the oil in a 10" skillet over medium heat. Add the garlic and cook, stirring often, for 2 minutes, or until golden.

✍ Add the fennel and cook, stirring often, for 10 minutes.

✍ Add the edamame, arugula or spinach, remaining ¾ teaspoon salt, and remaining ¼ teaspoon pepper and cook, stirring often, for 5 minutes, or until the spinach wilts.

✍ Add the tomatoes. Increase the heat to medium-high and cook for 5 minutes, or until the tomatoes have softened.

✍ To serve, preheat the oven to 400°F. Coat a jelly-roll pan with cooking spray. Use the foil to lift the polenta from the baking pan and invert it onto a cutting board. Turn the polenta right side up. With a short side facing you, cut the polenta lengthwise into 3 equal strips and crosswise into 4 equal strips.

✍ Place 6 pieces of polenta in the jelly-roll pan. Sprinkle each piece with 1 tablespoon mozzarella and top with ¼ cup of the vegetable mixture. Sprinkle each piece with another tablespoon smoked mozzarella. Place the remaining polenta pieces on top of each stack. Spoon ¼ cup of the vegetable mixture on top of each stack. Sprinkle each stack with 1 teaspoon of the Parmesan.

✍ Bake for 8–10 minutes, or until heated through.

Makes 6 servings

VEGETABLE HANDROLLS

1 cup shelled edamame

8 spears asparagus, blanched and halved
lengthwise

1 medium carrot, cut into matchsticks

⅓ English cucumber, cut into matchsticks

2 tablespoons soy sauce

3 tablespoons seasoned rice wine vinegar

1 tablespoon minced fresh ginger

1 teaspoon toasted sesame oil

¾ cup short-grain, sweet sticky rice

4 sheets nori (untoasted dried seaweed)

Soy sauce (optional)

Wasabi paste (optional)

Pickled ginger (optional)

Edamame

🌿 In a medium saucepan, bring 2 cups salted water to a boil over high heat. Add the edamame and return to a boil. Cook the edamame for 5–7 minutes, or until tender-crisp. Drain well.

🌿 In a bowl, combine the edamame, asparagus, carrot, cucumber, soy sauce, 1 tablespoon of the vinegar, ginger, and oil. Cover and marinate.

🌿 Rinse the rice with cool water several times until the water is clear. Drain well. In a small heavy saucepan, bring 1¼ cups cold water and the rice to a boil over high heat. Reduce the heat to low, cover, and simmer for 20 minutes, or until the water is absorbed. Do not lift the cover during the cooking time. Remove the pan from the heat and let stand, covered, for 10 minutes. Spoon the rice into a nonmetallic bowl. Stir in the remaining 2 tablespoons vinegar.

🌿 Meanwhile, carefully pass each sheet of nori over a gas flame or electric burner until it turns a bright green. With a short side facing you, using a scissor, cut each nori sheet crosswise in half. (You will have eight 7" × 4" pieces of nori.)

🌿 With the rough side up and a short side facing you, spoon ¼ cup of the rice in a 1"-wide strip across the middle of the nori sheet.

🌿 Arrange ⅛ of the edamame mixture on top of the rice. Spoon some of the marinade on top of the edamame mixture. Roll the nori up and around the filling to form a cone. Seal the cone by dipping your finger in water and rubbing it along the edge of the nori, pressing to seal. Repeat with the remaining nori, rice, edamame mixture, and marinade. Serve with the soy sauce, wasabi paste, and pickled ginger, if desired.

Makes 8 servings

SALADS

From side to main-dish salads,
colorful edamame add great
texture and zest to each dish

ROASTED ASPARAGUS SALAD

1 cup shelled, cooked edamame

1 bunch (1 pound) asparagus, trimmed

1 large red bell pepper, quartered

2 tablespoons sour cream

2 tablespoons extra-virgin olive oil

1 tablespoon fresh lemon juice

¼ teaspoon grated lemon peel

¼ teaspoon salt

⅛ teaspoon freshly ground black pepper

8 leaves red-leaf lettuce

¼ cup shredded Parmesan cheese

Rinse the edamame under cold running water and drain well.

Preheat the oven to 450°F. Line a baking sheet with foil and coat with olive oil cooking spray. Using a vegetable peeler, peel off the lower half of the asparagus stalks. Place the asparagus and bell pepper on the prepared sheet and bake for 22 minutes, or until the vegetables are tender-crisp. Set aside to cool.

When cool enough to handle, cut the asparagus into 1" lengths. Cut the bell pepper lengthwise into strips, then crosswise into 1" lengths.

In a medium bowl, whisk together the sour cream, oil, lemon juice, lemon peel, salt, and black pepper until smooth. Add the asparagus, bell pepper, and edamame and toss to coat well.

To serve, arrange the lettuce leaves on a serving platter. Spoon the vegetable mixture on top. Sprinkle on the cheese.

Makes 4 servings

BROCCOLI AND
CAULIFLOWER SALAD

1 cup shelled, cooked edamame

3 cups cauliflower florets, large florets cut into quarters

3 cups broccoli florets, large florets cut into quarters

1 orange bell pepper, chopped

2 tablespoons extra-virgin olive oil

1 teaspoon dry mustard

1 tablespoon light miso paste

2 tablespoons rice wine vinegar

1 tablespoon honey

¼ teaspoon salt

Rinse the edamame under cold running water and drain well.

Bring 1½ quarts water to a boil over high heat. Add the cauliflower and cook for 2 minutes. Add the broccoli and cook for 3 minutes, or until tender-crisp. Pour in a colander and rinse under cold running water. Drain well. Place in a large bowl, along with the pepper and edamame.

Meanwhile, in a large serving bowl, whisk together the oil, mustard, and miso until well blended. Stir in the vinegar, honey, and salt. Add the drained broccoli, cauliflower, pepper, and edamame and toss to coat well.

Makes 4 servings

GRILLED TOMATOES WITH EDAMAME AND GOAT CHEESE

Prep time: 20 minutes • Cook time: 10 minutes

Salad

1 cup shelled, cooked edamame

5 plum tomatoes, halved lengthwise

2 cups sliced escarole

2 cups sliced romaine lettuce

4 ounces goat cheese, crumbled

Dressing

½ teaspoon fennel seeds

3 tablespoons extra-virgin olive oil

2 tablespoons white wine vinegar

¼ teaspoon salt

⅛ teaspoon freshly ground black pepper

🌿 *To make the salad:* Rinse the edamame under cold running water and drain well. Preheat a grill pan set over medium-high heat. Coat the grill pan with olive oil cooking spray and place the tomatoes cut side down on the grill. Cook for 10 minutes, or until softened and charred, turning halfway during the cooking. Cut 8 of the tomato halves in half again lengthwise for the salad. Reserve the 2 remaining tomato halves for the dressing.

🌿 When ready to serve, combine the escarole and romaine and divide among 4 salad plates. Arrange 4 tomato wedges in a spoke fashion on each salad. Evenly divide the edamame and cheese on the plates. Drizzle with the dressing.

🌿 *To make the dressing:* Crush the fennel seeds in a mortar and pestle (or place in a small plastic food bag and crush with a small, heavy skillet). Place the fennel in a mini food processor or blender. Peel the skin from the 2 reserved tomato halves and place the tomato flesh in the food processor or blender. Add the oil, vinegar, salt, and pepper. Process or blend until smooth.

Makes 4 servings

FRISÉE SALAD WITH PANCETTA AND SEARED SHALLOTS

Prep time: 20 minutes • Cook time: 10 minutes
PHOTOGRAPH ON PAGE 59

¼ cup extra-virgin olive oil

12 shallots, peeled with root ends intact and halved lengthwise

2 ounces lean pancetta or lean slab bacon, cut into ¼" dice

1 cup shelled, cooked edamame

3 tablespoons fresh orange juice

1 tablespoon red wine vinegar

¼ teaspoon sugar

⅛ teaspoon freshly ground black pepper

2 cups frisée lettuce or arugula, torn into bite-size pieces

2 cups Boston lettuce, torn into bite-size pieces

Heat the oil in a medium skillet over medium heat. Add the shallots and cook, stirring occasionally, for 5 minutes, or until tender-crisp. Add the pancetta or bacon and cook for 5 minutes, or until the pancetta or bacon is golden brown, stirring occasionally.

Remove the pan from the heat. Remove the meat and shallots with a slotted spoon and place in a medium bowl along with the edamame. Add the orange juice, vinegar, sugar, and pepper to the skillet, scraping the bottom to remove any flavorful bits.

Evenly divide the frisée or arugula and Boston lettuce onto 4 salad plates. Top each with one-quarter of the shallot mixture and drizzle with the dressing. Serve immediately.

Makes 4 servings

MUSTARDY POTATO SALAD

Prep time: 10 minutes • Cook time: 15 minutes

1½ pounds red potatoes, cut into 1" cubes

1 small red onion, chopped

⅓ cup mayonnaise

⅓ cup plain yogurt

1 tablespoon grainy mustard

1 tablespoon cider vinegar

1 tablespoon chopped fresh tarragon

½ teaspoon salt

½ teaspoon freshly ground black pepper

1 cup shelled, cooked edamame

1 large rib celery, chopped

🌿 In a large saucepan, bring 1½ quarts water to a boil over high heat. Add the potatoes and cook for 15 minutes, or until tender when pierced with a knife. Stir in the onion, remove from the heat, and drain well.

🌿 In a large bowl, combine the mayonnaise, yogurt, mustard, vinegar, tarragon, salt, and pepper. Add the drained potatoes, edamame, and celery and toss to coat well. Serve warm or refrigerate to serve cold.

Makes 6 servings

ROASTED PORTOBELLO
AND SHALLOT SALAD

¾ cup shelled, cooked edamame

3 small portobello mushrooms, stems removed

¼ cup extra-virgin olive oil

3 tablespoons sherry or red wine vinegar

12 shallots, peeled with root ends intact and
    halved lengthwise

1½ teaspoons chopped fresh sage

¼ teaspoon salt

¼ teaspoon freshly ground black pepper

6 cups baby spinach or arugula

🌿 Rinse the edamame under cold running water and drain well.

🌿 Preheat the oven to 400°F. Line a baking sheet with foil and coat the foil with olive oil cooking spray. Using a tablespoon, scrape out the dark gills from underneath the mushrooms and discard. In a small dish, stir together 1 tablespoon each of the oil and sherry or vinegar. Brush both sides of the mushrooms with the mixture and set right side up on the baking sheet, along with the shallots.

🌿 Bake for 20 minutes, turning and basting once with the oil-vinegar mixture, or until the shallots and mushrooms are tender when pierced. Place the baking sheet on a rack to cool. When cool enough to handle, halve the mushrooms and cut crosswise into ½"-thick slices.

🌿 Place 8 of the shallot halves in a blender or mini food processor. Add the sage, salt, pepper, and remaining oil and sherry or vinegar. Blend or process until smooth.

🌿 Place the spinach or arugula on 4 salad plates. Evenly divide the mushrooms, shallots, and edamame onto the plates. Drizzle with the shallot dressing.

Makes 4 servings

TABBOULEH SALAD
WITH MINT AND BASIL

¾ cup bulgur wheat

2 cups boiling water

¾ cup shelled, cooked edamame

1 medium cucumber, peeled, seeded, and chopped

2 medium tomatoes, chopped

3 scallions, thinly sliced

1 cup fresh basil, chopped

½ cup fresh mint, chopped

¼ cup fresh lemon juice

3 tablespoons extra-virgin olive oil

½ teaspoon salt

¼ teaspoon freshly ground black pepper

In a medium bowl, combine the bulgur and boiling water. Let stand for 30 minutes, or until softened. Drain the bulgur through a fine mesh sieve and shake out any excess water.

In a large bowl, combine the edamame, cucumber, tomatoes, scallions, basil, mint, lemon juice, oil, salt, pepper, and drained bulgur. Cover and refrigerate for at least 1 hour.

Makes 6 servings

LEBANESE PITA SALAD

1 cup shelled, cooked edamame

½ small red onion, chopped

2 whole wheat pitas (4" each)

3 medium ripe tomatoes, chopped

1 yellow bell pepper, chopped

⅓ cup fresh basil, chopped

⅓ cup fresh mint, chopped

3 tablespoons extra-virgin olive oil

2 tablespoons fresh lemon juice

1 clove garlic, crushed

½ teaspoon ground cumin

½ teaspoon salt

¼ teaspoon freshly ground black pepper

Rinse the edamame under cold running water and drain well.

Place the onion in a bowl and add 2 cups hot tap water to cover. Let stand at least 15 minutes.

Meanwhile, toast the pitas on the lowest setting to dry them out. When cool enough to handle, split the pitas in half and cut or tear the pitas into ¾" pieces (you should have 2 cups).

In a large bowl, toss together the tomatoes, bell pepper, edamame, basil, mint, oil, lemon juice, garlic, cumin, salt, and black pepper. Drain the onion well and add to the bowl, along with the pitas. Toss to combine well.

Makes 4 servings

SESAME-GINGER COUSCOUS SALAD

Prep time: 20 minutes • Cook time: 9 minutes

PHOTOGRAPH ON PAGE 59

1 cup shelled, cooked edamame

1 cup (4 ounces) Israeli couscous (pearl pasta; see note)

1½ cups pea pods, trimmed, stringed, and halved crosswise

1 cup grape tomatoes, halved

2 tablespoons rice wine vinegar

2 tablespoons apple juice or water

1 tablespoon + 1½ teaspoons sesame-ginger stir-fry sauce

2 teaspoons toasted sesame oil

1 teaspoon honey

1 slice (¼") fresh ginger

¼ teaspoon salt

Edamame

🌿 Rinse the edamame under cold running water and drain well.

🌿 In a large saucepan, bring 2 quarts water to a boil over high heat. Add the couscous and cook for 8 minutes, or until al dente. Add the pea pods and cook for 1 minute. Pour into a colander and rinse under cold running water. Drain well and place in a large bowl. Add the tomatoes and edamame.

🌿 In a blender, blend the vinegar, apple juice or water, stir-fry sauce, oil, honey, ginger, and salt until smooth. Add to the couscous mixture and toss to coat well.

Note: You may substitute an equal weight of orzo for the Israeli couscous. Cook the orzo according to package directions.

Makes 6 servings

COBB SALAD WITH EDAMAME

Dressing

- 4 tablespoons extra-virgin olive oil
- 3 tablespoons red wine vinegar
- 2 shallots, finely chopped
- ¼ teaspoon freshly ground black pepper
- ⅓ cup crumbled Gorgonzola or blue cheese, divided

Salad

- 1 cup shelled, cooked edamame
- 8 cups sliced romaine lettuce or mixed salad greens
- 8 ounces roasted turkey breast, coarsely chopped
- 1 small avocado, pitted, peeled, and cut into ¾" cubes
- ¾ cup grape or cherry tomatoes, halved
- ½ red onion, halved lengthwise and thinly sliced
- 4 slices bacon, cooked and crumbled

To make the dressing: In a small bowl, whisk together the oil, vinegar, shallots, and pepper. Stir in 2 tablespoons of the cheese.

To make the salad: Rinse the edamame under cold running water and drain well. Place the greens on a serving platter or in 4 large shallow bowls. Arrange the turkey, avocado, edamame, tomatoes, and onion in a decorative pattern on top of the greens. Sprinkle on the bacon and the remaining cheese. Serve the salad with the dressing on the side.

Makes 4 servings

WARM SCALLOP
AND EDAMAME SALAD

1 pound sea scallops, side muscle removed and patted dry with paper towels

1½ teaspoons grated lemon peel

¼ teaspoon salt

¼ teaspoon freshly ground black pepper

6 cups mesclun or spring mix

3 tablespoons extra-virgin olive oil

1 yellow bell pepper, cut into thin strips

1 cup shelled, cooked edamame

3 tablespoons white balsamic or white wine vinegar

2 tablespoons finely chopped chives or scallions

In a medium bowl, toss together the scallops, 1 teaspoon of the lemon peel, salt, and black pepper. Divide the greens among 4 salad plates.

Heat the oil in a large skillet over medium-high heat. Add the scallops and cook for 2–3 minutes, turning when the scallops are browned and cooking just until they turn opaque. Do not overcook. Remove the pan from the heat. Using a slotted spoon, place the scallops on a plate and cover the scallops with foil to keep warm.

Add the bell pepper and edamame to the skillet and cook for 7 minutes, stirring occasionally, until tender-crisp. Stir in the vinegar, remaining ½ teaspoon lemon peel, and the chives or scallions and cook, stirring to break up the brown bits. Add the scallops and any collected juice to the skillet and stir to blend. Evenly divide the scallop mixture over the greens. Serve immediately.

Makes 4 servings

SOUPS

From thin broths to cream soups,
edamame add a unique richness
to every spoonful

SUMMER GARDEN VEGETABLE SOUP

2 tablespoons extra-virgin olive oil

3 large cloves garlic, minced

1 leek, trimmed, halved lengthwise, and sliced

1 large carrot, halved lengthwise and sliced

1 bulb fennel, trimmed (reserving fronds), cored, and chopped

1 large tomato, chopped

1 medium zucchini, quartered lengthwise and sliced

1 ear corn, kernels cut from the cob

1½ cups shelled edamame

4½ cups vegetable broth

1 cup carrot juice

1 tablespoon + 1 teaspoon minced fresh thyme or lemon thyme

½ teaspoon salt

¼ teaspoon freshly ground black pepper

2 cups baby spinach

1 tablespoon + 1½ teaspoons minced fresh parsley

1 teaspoon grated lemon peel

Edamame

🌿 Heat the oil in a large saucepan over medium heat. Add the garlic and leek and cook for 3 minutes, stirring occasionally.

🌿 Add the carrot and fennel and cook for 5 minutes.

🌿 Add the tomato, zucchini, corn, and edamame and cook, stirring occasionally, for 5 minutes.

🌿 Add the broth, juice, 1 tablespoon of the thyme, salt, and pepper and bring to a boil. Reduce the heat to low and simmer, stirring occasionally, for 15 minutes, or until the vegetables are tender. Stir in the spinach and cook for 5 minutes, or until the spinach wilts.

🌿 Meanwhile, finely chop enough of the reserved fennel fronds to measure 1½ tablespoons. Place in a small bowl. Add the remaining 1 teaspoon thyme, parsley, and lemon peel.

🌿 To serve, ladle the soup into bowls. Sprinkle some of the fennel-lemon mixture into each bowl of soup.

Makes 8 servings

TUSCAN MINESTRONE WITH ORZO

Prep time: 20 minutes • Cook time: 45 minutes

1 tablespoon extra-virgin olive oil

¼ pound piece prosciutto, chopped

4 large cloves garlic, minced

2 medium carrots, halved lengthwise and sliced

2 ribs celery, diagonally sliced

1 small red onion, chopped

¼ pound savoy cabbage, cored and sliced

¼ pound Swiss chard, trimmed and sliced

1½ cups shelled edamame

6 cups beef broth or chicken broth

1 baking potato, peeled and cut into ½" pieces

1 tablespoon tomato paste

½ teaspoon salt

¼ teaspoon freshly ground black pepper

½ cup orzo

Grated Parmesan cheese

🌿 Heat the oil in a large saucepan over medium heat. Add the prosciutto and cook, stirring often, for 5 minutes, or until lightly browned.

🌿 Add the garlic, carrots, celery, and onion and cook, stirring occasionally, for 10 minutes.

🌿 Add the cabbage, Swiss chard, and edamame and cook for 5 minutes, stirring occasionally, or until the cabbage and Swiss chard have wilted.

🌿 Add the broth, potato, tomato paste, salt, and pepper and bring to a boil. Reduce the heat to low and simmer for 15 minutes, stirring occasionally. Add the orzo and cook for 10 minutes, or until the vegetables and orzo are tender.

🌿 Serve the soup with the cheese.

Makes 8 servings

CREAM OF GARLIC EDAMAME SOUP

Prep time: 15 minutes • Cook time: 55 minutes

2 tablespoons extra-virgin olive oil

1 bulb garlic (2¾ ounces), separated into cloves and peeled

2 bay leaves

3 cups shelled edamame

5 cups chicken broth

¼ teaspoon salt

¼ teaspoon freshly ground black pepper

1 cup heavy cream

🍃 Heat the oil in a large saucepan over medium-low heat. Add the garlic and bay leaves and cook, stirring occasionally, for 10 minutes, or until softened and golden.

🍃 Add the edamame and cook, stirring occasionally, for 5 minutes.

🍃 Add the broth, salt, and pepper. Bring to a boil over high heat. Reduce the heat to low, partially cover, and simmer for 35 minutes, or until tender.

🍃 Remove and discard the bay leaves. In a blender or food processor, blend or process the soup in batches until smooth. Return the soup to the saucepan. Stir in the cream. Heat the soup over medium heat until heated through.

Makes 6 servings

SAVORY MUSHROOM TART ❦ PAGE 22

55

CURRIED
CROQUETTES
PAGE 26

VEGETABLE HANDROLLS PAGE 30

SIMPLE BRUSCHETTA 🌿 PAGE 24 (top)
ROASTED EDAMAME 🌿 PAGE 13 (bottom)

57

ROASTED ASPARAGUS SALAD 🌿 PAGE 34

FRISÉE SALAD
WITH PANCETTA
AND SEARED
SHALLOTS
PAGE 38

SESAME-GINGER COUSCOUS SALAD PAGE 44

CHICKEN
TORTILLA
SOUP
PAGE 76

WARM SCALLOP AND EDAMAME SALAD PAGE 47

HEARTY VEGETABLE BEEF SOUP 🌿 PAGE 74 (top)
THAI SEAFOOD SOUP 🌿 PAGE 78 (bottom)

61

SUMMER GARDEN VEGETABLE SOUP 🌿 PAGE 50

VEGGIE BURGERS
PAGE 87

PENNE WITH EDAMAME AND GOAT CHEESE SAUCE PAGE 89

ROSEMARY LAMB KEBABS ON COUSCOUS   PAGE 108

64

SEA BASS EN
PAPILLOTE
PAGE 98

ASIAN SALMON AND
WASABI MASHED POTATOES PAGE 96

GRILLED FLANK STEAK WITH

JEWELED SALSA 🌿 PAGE 104

ORANGE BEEF
STIR-FRY
✍ PAGE 106

BALSAMIC-GLAZED PORK CHOPS ✍ PAGE 103

CREAMY RISOTTO ✿ PAGE 123

BALSAMIC-GLAZED
WINTER VEGETABLES
🌿 PAGE 112

SUCCOTASH WITH OKRA AND EDAMAME 🌿 PAGE 116

GREEN BEANS AND EDAMAME À LA GRECQUE PAGE 117

CORN AND EDAMAME CHOWDER

Prep time: 20 minutes • Cook time: 45 minutes

¼ pound sliced bacon, chopped

1 medium green bell pepper, chopped

1 medium red bell pepper, chopped

1 medium onion, chopped

4 cups chicken broth

2 small sweet potatoes (14 ounces), cut into ½" pieces

1½ cups shelled edamame

½ teaspoon salt

½ teaspoon freshly ground black pepper

2 cans (14.75 ounces each) creamed corn

¼ cup heavy cream

In a large saucepan over medium heat, cook the bacon for 8 minutes, stirring occasionally, or until browned and crisp. With a slotted spoon, remove the bacon to a paper towel to drain. Pour off all but 3 tablespoons of drippings from the saucepan.

Add the bell peppers and onion and cook, stirring occasionally, for 10 minutes.

Add the broth, sweet potatoes, edamame, salt, and black pepper and bring to a boil over high heat. Reduce the heat to low and simmer, stirring occasionally, for 20 minutes, or until tender. Stir in the creamed corn and cream and cook for 5 minutes, or until heated through. Serve topped with the chopped bacon.

Makes 8 servings

MISO EDAMAME SOUP

Prep time: 15 minutes • Cook time: 20 minutes

8 cups water

1 cup shelled edamame

1 piece wakame (4")

1 piece kombu (4" × 1")

1 cup loosely packed bonito flakes

⅓ cup aka (red) miso

1 small red bell pepper, diced

2 ounces shiitake mushrooms, stems removed and sliced

¼ pound soft tofu, cut into ½" pieces

2 scallions, diagonally sliced

In a medium saucepan, bring 2 cups salted water to a boil over high heat. Add the edamame and cook for 5 minutes. Drain the edamame well and set aside.

Place the wakame in a bowl with 2 cups cold water. Let the wakame soak for 15 minutes, or until rehydrated and softened. Remove the wakame and discard the water. Cut away the ribs and slice the wakame crosswise into ½" pieces. Set aside.

Using a damp cloth, wipe the kombu. Place the kombu in a medium saucepan with 4 cups water over medium-high heat and bring almost to a boil. Remove kombu and discard. Add the bonito flakes to the stock and remove the saucepan from the heat. Do not stir. Let the bonito flakes sink to the bottom of the saucepan. Pour the stock into a sieve placed over a bowl. Discard the bonito flakes.

Place 1 cup of the stock back into the saucepan over medium-high heat. Add the miso and stir until thoroughly combined. Add the remaining stock, reserved wakame, pepper, and mushrooms and simmer for 3 minutes, or until the vegetables have softened. Stir in the reserved edamame, tofu, and scallions. Heat through but do not boil.

Makes 4 servings

HEARTY VEGETABLE
BEEF SOUP

Prep time: 25 minutes • Cook time: 2 hours and 15 minutes
PHOTOGRAPH ON PAGE 61

¼ ounce dried porcini mushrooms (about ⅓ cup)

2 tablespoons extra-virgin olive oil

2 pounds bottom beef round, cut into 1" cubes

4 large cloves garlic, minced

2 medium carrots, halved lengthwise and sliced

1 medium onion, chopped

½ bulb fennel, trimmed, cored, and chopped

2 bay leaves

½ pound cremini mushrooms, sliced

1½ cups shelled edamame

4 cups beef broth

4 cups water

½ teaspoon salt

¼ teaspoon freshly ground black pepper

1 cup barley

🌿 Soak the porcini in ½ cup hot water for 20 minutes, or until rehydrated and softened. Remove the mushrooms from the liquid and chop. Reserve the mushrooms and the liquid.

🌿 Meanwhile, heat the oil in a large saucepan over medium-high heat. Add the beef and brown, turning occasionally, about 15 minutes. Remove the beef to a plate.

🌿 In the drippings in the saucepan over medium heat, cook the garlic, stirring often, for 2 minutes. Add the carrots, onion, fennel, and bay leaves and cook, stirring often, for 10 minutes. Add the cremini, edamame, and reserved porcini and cook, stirring often, for 5 minutes.

🌿 Add the beef, broth, water, reserved porcini liquid, salt, and pepper and bring to a boil over high heat. Reduce the heat to low, partially cover, and simmer, stirring occasionally, for 1 hour. Add the barley and simmer for 45 minutes, or until the meat and barley are tender.

🌿 Remove and discard the bay leaves.

Makes 8 servings

CHICKEN TORTILLA SOUP

Prep time: 35 minutes • Cook time: 50 minutes
PHOTOGRAPH ON PAGE 60

2 tablespoons extra-virgin olive oil

2 boneless, skinless chicken breast halves

4 cups chicken broth

2 dried ancho chile peppers (1¼ ounces) (wear plastic gloves when handling)

1 small onion, chopped

3 large cloves garlic, minced

1½ cups shelled edamame

2 small yellow squash and/or zucchini, quartered lengthwise and sliced

2 cans (14.5 ounces each) peeled diced tomatoes seasoned with mild chiles

1 tablespoon chopped fresh oregano

½ teaspoon salt

¼ cup fresh cilantro, chopped

4 corn tortillas (6" each), cut into thin strips

½ cup shredded Monterey Jack cheese

🌿 Preheat the oven to 350°F.

🌿 Heat the oil in a large saucepan over medium heat. Add the chicken breasts and cook for 15 minutes, or until a thermometer inserted in the thickest portion registers 160°F and the juices run clear. Remove the chicken to a plate. Reserve the drippings in the saucepan.

🌿 Meanwhile, bring 2 cups of the broth to a boil. Add the ancho chiles and remove from the heat. Let the chiles soak for 20 minutes until re-hydrated and softened. Remove the chiles from the broth. Reserve the broth. Remove the stems and seeds from the chiles and chop.

🌿 Place the chiles in a blender or food processor. Strain the reserved broth and place in the blender or food processor. Blend or process for 1 minute. Place a sieve over a bowl. Pour the chile mixture into the sieve. Discard the solids and reserve the liquid.

🌿 In the drippings remaining in the saucepan, cook the onion and garlic over medium heat, stirring often, for 8 minutes.

🌿 Add the edamame and squash and cook, stirring often, for 5 minutes.

🌿 Add the reserved liquid, remaining broth, tomatoes (with juice), oregano, and salt and bring to a boil over high heat. Reduce the heat to low and simmer, stirring occasionally, for 10 minutes.

🌿 Shred the cooked chicken and stir into the soup with the cilantro and heat through.

🌿 Coat the tortillas with olive oil cooking spray and place on a large baking sheet. Bake for 8 minutes, or until lightly toasted.

🌿 To serve, ladle the soup into bowls and place a few tortilla strips and some cheese in each bowl.

Makes 8 servings

THAI SEAFOOD SOUP

1 pound medium shrimp

2 tablespoons vegetable oil

4 large cloves garlic, minced

8 cups water

2 tablespoons minced fresh ginger

2 Thai chile peppers, seeded (wear plastic gloves when handling) and sliced (see note)

1 large carrot, halved lengthwise and sliced

1½ cups shelled edamame

1 cup straw mushrooms, drained and rinsed

¼ cup fresh lime juice

2 tablespoons sliced lemongrass

2 tablespoons fish sauce (nam pla)

1 dozen mussels, scrubbed and debearded

¼ cup fresh cilantro, chopped

🌿 Peel the shrimp, reserving the shells. Devein the shrimp and reserve.

🌿 Heat 1 tablespoon of the oil in a large saucepan over medium heat. Add the reserved shrimp shells and 1 tablespoon of the garlic and cook, stirring often, for 3–4 minutes, or until fragrant.

🌿 Add the water and 1 tablespoon of the ginger and bring to a boil over high heat. Reduce the heat to low and simmer for 15 minutes. Place a sieve over a large bowl. Pour the stock into the sieve to strain out the shells. Discard the shells. Wipe the saucepan clean.

🌿 Heat the remaining 1 tablespoon oil in the same saucepan over medium heat. Add the remaining garlic and ginger and the chiles and cook, stirring often, for 2 minutes.

🌿 Add the carrot and edamame and cook, stirring often, for 5 minutes.

🌿 Add the reserved stock, mushrooms, lime juice, lemongrass, and fish sauce and bring to a boil over high heat. Reduce the heat to medium and cook, stirring occasionally, for 10 minutes.

🌿 Add the mussels and cook for 3 minutes. Add the reserved shrimp and cook, stirring often, for 5 minutes, or until the mussels have opened and the shrimp are opaque.

🌿 Stir in the cilantro.

Note: If you prefer more heat in your food, do not remove the seeds from the chile peppers.

Makes 6 servings

TWIN PUREED SOUPS

Prep time: 30 minutes • Cook time: 55 minutes

3 tablespoons extra-virgin olive oil

1 large onion, chopped

1 teaspoon curry powder

1 butternut squash (1¼ pounds), peeled, seeded, and cut into 1" pieces

1¼ teaspoons salt

6½ cups chicken broth

1 tablespoon + 1½ teaspoons minced fresh ginger

2 cups shelled edamame

1 cup heavy cream

¼ cup fresh cilantro, chopped

Plain yogurt (for garnish)

Cilantro sprig (for garnish)

Edamame

80

🌿 Heat 1 tablespoon of the oil in a medium saucepan over medium heat. Add half the onion and cook, stirring occasionally, for 5 minutes.

🌿 Add the curry powder and cook, stirring often, for 1 minute. Add the squash and ½ teaspoon of the salt and cook, stirring occasionally, for 5 minutes.

🌿 Add 2 cups of the broth and bring to a boil over high heat. Reduce the heat to low, partially cover, and simmer for 25 minutes, or until the squash is tender. Place the squash mixture in batches in a blender or food processor. Blend or process until smooth. Return the squash soup to the saucepan and keep warm.

🌿 Meanwhile, in another medium saucepan, heat the remaining 2 tablespoons oil over medium heat. Add the remaining onion and ginger and cook, stirring occasionally, for 5 minutes.

🌿 Add the edamame and the remaining 4½ cups broth and ¾ teaspoon salt and bring to a boil over high heat. Reduce the heat to low, partially cover, and simmer for 35 minutes, or until very tender.

🌿 Place the edamame mixture in batches in a blender or food processor. Blend or process until smooth.

🌿 Return the edamame puree to the saucepan and stir in the cream. Heat over medium heat and simmer, stirring occasionally, for 5 minutes. Stir in the cilantro.

🌿 To serve, pour about 1 cup of the edamame soup into a bowl or soup plate. Pour about ½ cup of the squash soup into the center of the edamame soup. Using a wooden skewer or thin knife, drag or pull the squash soup through the edamame soup in a pretty design. Garnish with a dollop of yogurt and a cilantro sprig.

Makes 6 servings

SOUPE AU PISTOU

Puree

- ½ cup shelled edamame
- ½ cup fresh basil
- ¼ cup grated Parmesan cheese
- ¼ cup tomato paste
- 1 tablespoon extra-virgin olive oil

Soup

- 2 tablespoons extra-virgin olive oil
- 1 medium onion, chopped
- 2 cups shelled edamame
- 1 large tomato, chopped
- 1 medium yellow squash, halved lengthwise and sliced
- 6 cups vegetable broth
- ½ pound red potatoes, cut into ½" pieces
- ¼ pound green beans, trimmed and cut into 1" pieces
- ¼ pound linguine, broken into 2" pieces
- ½ teaspoon salt

🌿 *To make the puree:* In a medium saucepan, bring 2 cups salted water to a boil over high heat. Add the edamame and cook for 5 minutes. Drain the edamame well and place in a blender or food processor with the basil, cheese, tomato paste, and oil. Blend or process until almost smooth. Set aside.

🌿 *To make the soup:* Heat the oil in a large saucepan over medium heat. Add the onion and cook for 5 minutes, stirring occasionally.

🌿 Add the edamame, tomato, and squash and cook, stirring occasionally, for 5 minutes.

🌿 Add the broth, potatoes, beans, linguine, and salt. Bring to a boil over high heat. Reduce the heat to low and simmer for 20 minutes, or until the vegetables are tender. Stir in the reserved puree and heat through.

Makes 8 servings

MAIN DISHES

From grilled roasts to delicate fish
dishes, edamame are highlighted in
these hearty entrées

VEGETABLE CHILI

1 cup uncooked brown rice

2 tablespoons extra-virgin olive oil

2 large carrots, chopped

1 large onion, chopped

1 red bell pepper, chopped

1 clove garlic, minced

1 teaspoon ground cumin

1 tablespoon chili powder

2 cups vegetable broth

1 can (14.75 ounces) creamed corn

1 can (14–19 ounces) black beans, rinsed and drained

2 cups shelled edamame

¼ cup fresh cilantro, chopped

Sour cream (optional)

🌿 Prepare the rice according to package directions.

🌿 Meanwhile, heat the oil in a large saucepan over high heat. Add the carrots, onion, and pepper and cook for 7 minutes, or until browned. Add the garlic, cumin, and chili powder and cook for 1 minute.

🌿 Add the broth and creamed corn and bring to a boil over high heat. Reduce the heat to low and simmer for 20 minutes. Add the beans and edamame and cook for 7 minutes, or until the edamame is tender. Stir in the cilantro.

🌿 Serve with rice. Add a dollop of sour cream, if using.

Makes 4 servings

VEGGIE BURGERS

1½ cups shelled edamame

1 small red onion, minced

1 carrot, grated

1 clove garlic, minced

½ cup dried bread crumbs

1 egg, beaten

½ cup shredded Jarlsberg cheese

½ teaspoon salt

¼ teaspoon freshly ground black pepper

2 tablespoons extra-virgin olive oil

4 whole grain rolls

4 teaspoons honey mustard

4 slices tomato

¼ cup shredded lettuce

Place the edamame in a small saucepan with 2 cups salted water. Bring to a boil over high heat. Reduce the heat to medium-low, cover, and simmer for 10 minutes. Drain well and cool slightly.

Place the edamame in a food processor and pulse until lightly mashed. Place in a bowl with the onion, carrot, garlic, bread crumbs, egg, cheese, salt, and pepper and gently toss to combine well. Shape into 4 burgers.

Heat the oil in a large skillet over medium-high heat. Add the burgers and cook for 5 minutes, or until golden and cooked through, turning once.

Place a burger on each roll and spread with the mustard. Top with the tomato and lettuce.

Makes 4 servings

THAI VEGETABLE BOWL

2 tablespoons vegetable oil

1 carrot, finely chopped

1 rib celery, finely chopped

1 clove garlic, minced

4 cups vegetable broth

1 can (13.5 ounces) light coconut milk

¼ teaspoon green curry paste

1½ cups shelled edamame

8 ounces rice noodles or buckwheat noodles

1 package (8 ounces) smoked tofu, cubed

2 tablespoons sliced fresh basil

Heat the oil in a large saucepan over medium-high heat. Add the carrot, celery, and garlic and cook for 5 minutes. Add the broth, coconut milk, curry paste, edamame, and noodles and bring to a boil over high heat. Reduce the heat to medium-low and cook for 10 minutes, or until the noodles are al dente.

Stir in the tofu and basil and cook for 2 minutes, or until heated through.

Makes 4 servings

PENNE WITH EDAMAME AND GOAT CHEESE SAUCE

Prep time: 25 minutes • Cook time: 16 minutes
PHOTOGRAPH ON PAGE 63

⅓ cup dry-packed sun-dried tomato halves (10 halves)

¾ pound penne

1 cup shelled edamame

2 tablespoons extra-virgin olive oil

2 leeks (white and pale green end only), rinsed well and sliced

1½ cups half-and-half

½ cup (2½ ounces) fresh goat cheese, crumbled

1 cup grape or small cherry tomatoes, halved

½ cup grated Parmesan cheese

½ cup fresh basil, slivered

Soften the sun-dried tomatoes in 1 cup boiling water for 10 minutes. Drain well and cut crosswise into slivers. Prepare the pasta according to package directions, adding the edamame during the last 7 minutes of the cooking. Reserve 1 cup of the pasta water for the sauce and drain the pasta and edamame in a colander.

Meanwhile, heat the oil in a skillet over medium heat. Add the leeks and cook for 5 minutes, stirring occasionally until softened. Add the half-and-half and bring to a simmer over medium heat. Simmer for 5 minutes, or until slightly thickened. Stir in the goat cheese and the sun-dried tomatoes and cook for 1 minute, or until thickened. Stir in the grape or cherry tomatoes and the Parmesan.

In a large bowl, combine the pasta and edamame, vegetable sauce mixture, and basil in a large pasta bowl. Toss until well blended. If the pasta absorbs the sauce, gradually add enough of the reserved pasta water until creamy.

Makes 4 servings

PASTA PRIMAVERA

    3 tablespoons pine nuts

    4 cloves garlic, peeled

    1 pound frozen or shelf-stable mini ravioli or
      tortellini

    2 carrots, thinly sliced

    1 bunch broccoli, cut into florets

    1 red bell pepper, chopped

    1 cup shelled edamame

 1½ cups fresh basil

  ⅓ cup chicken broth

  ⅓ cup grated Parmesan cheese + additional for
      serving

    2 tablespoons extra-virgin olive oil

  ½ teaspoon salt

  ¼ teaspoon freshly ground black pepper

✤ Place the pine nuts in a small dry skillet over medium heat, stirring frequently, for 2–3 minutes, or until lightly colored and fragrant. Set aside on a small plate to cool.

✤ Thread the garlic cloves on the end of a 10" skewer. Bring a large pot of water to a boil over high heat. Cook the pasta according to package directions, adding the carrots, broccoli, bell pepper, and edamame during the last 7 minutes of the cooking.

✤ While the pasta cooks, place the garlic skewer in the pot and cook for 5 minutes. Remove the skewer and place the garlic in a mini food processor or blender. Add the basil, broth, Parmesan, oil, salt, and pepper. Process or blend the basil pesto mixture until it is smooth.

✤ Drain the pasta and vegetables well and place them in a large serving bowl. Add the basil pesto and toss to coat well. Sprinkle with the pine nuts and serve with additional Parmesan, if you wish.

Makes 4 servings

PASTA WITH SWISS CHARD
AND RICOTTA

Prep time: 25 minutes • Cook time: 15 minutes

¼ cup pine nuts

¾ pound mini rigatoni

2 tablespoons extra-virgin olive oil

3 cloves garlic, minced

1 yellow bell pepper, chopped

1 bunch (¾ pound) Swiss chard, stems and leaves
  separated and chopped

1 cup shelled edamame

¼ teaspoon salt

¼ teaspoon crushed red-pepper flakes

¾ cup ricotta cheese

⅓ cup grated Parmesan cheese + additional for
  serving

Edamame

92

🌿 Place the pine nuts in a small dry skillet over medium heat, stirring frequently, for 2–3 minutes, or until lightly colored and fragrant. Set aside on a small plate to cool.

🌿 Prepare the pasta according to package directions, reserving 1 cup of the pasta water to use for the sauce.

🌿 Meanwhile, heat the oil in a large skillet over medium-low heat. Add the garlic, bell pepper, and chard stems. Cook for 8 minutes, stirring occasionally, until softened. Add the edamame, chard leaves, salt, and red-pepper flakes. Cook for 6 minutes, stirring frequently, until wilted and tender-crisp.

🌿 Puree the ricotta, Parmesan, and ⅓ cup of the reserved pasta water in a mini food processor or blender until smooth. In a large bowl, toss the drained pasta, vegetables, and ricotta mixture until combined. If needed, add additional pasta water to moisten the pasta. Sprinkle with the pine nuts and serve with additional Parmesan, if desired.

Makes 4 servings

VEGETABLE LASAGNA

2 tablespoons extra-virgin olive oil

1 bulb fennel, trimmed, cored, and thinly sliced

1 large red bell pepper, thinly sliced

2 zucchini, halved lengthwise and sliced

2 cloves garlic, finely chopped

1 cup shelled edamame

¾ teaspoon salt

2½ cups whole milk

8 ounces ricotta cheese

¼ cup all-purpose flour

½ teaspoon dried thyme, crushed

¼ teaspoon crushed fennel seed

¾ cup grated Parmesan cheese

6 no-boil lasagna noodles (7" × 3½")

1 cup shredded mozzarella cheese

🌿 Preheat the oven to 375°F. Coat an 8" × 8" baking dish with olive oil cooking spray.

🌿 Heat the oil in a large skillet over medium heat. Add the fennel, pepper, zucchini, and garlic and cook for 5 minutes, stirring occasionally. Add the edamame and ½ teaspoon of the salt and cook, stirring occasionally, for 7 minutes, or until the vegetables are just tender. Place the vegetables in a bowl and set aside.

🌿 In a blender, combine the milk, ricotta, flour, thyme, fennel seed, and remaining ¼ teaspoon salt and blend until smooth. Pour into the same skillet (no need to clean it) set over medium heat and bring to a simmer, stirring constantly. Cook for 2 minutes, or until thickened. Remove from the heat and stir in ½ cup of the Parmesan.

🌿 Spoon ½ cup of the cheese sauce into the prepared baking dish. Place 2 lasagna noodles (side by side) in the pan. Spoon half of the vegetables on top and spread in an even layer to cover the noodles. Drizzle with ½ cup sauce. Repeat with 2 noodles, the remaining vegetables, and ½ cup sauce. Sprinkle on ½ cup of the mozzarella and top with 2 lasagna noodles. Spoon the remaining 1½ cups sauce on top (it will go over the sides as well). Cover tightly with foil.

🌿 Bake for 45 minutes, or until hot in the center (an instant-read thermometer inserted in the center should read 180°F). Sprinkle the remaining ¼ cup Parmesan and ½ cup mozzarella evenly on top. Cover with foil and let stand for 20 minutes before serving.

Makes 6 servings

ASIAN SALMON AND
WASABI MASHED POTATOES

Prep time: 10 minutes • Cook time: 20 minutes
PHOTOGRAPH ON PAGE 65

2 tablespoons soy sauce

1 tablespoon toasted sesame oil

1 tablespoon freshly grated ginger

4 skinned salmon fillets (about 6 ounces each)

2 pounds Yukon gold potatoes, cut into 2" pieces

1 cup half-and-half or whole milk

3 tablespoons butter

2 teaspoons wasabi paste (see note)

½ teaspoon salt

1 cup shelled, cooked edamame

🌿 In a small bowl, combine the soy sauce, oil, and ginger. Place the salmon fillets on a plate and brush with the soy sauce mixture. Let stand at room temperature.

🌿 Lightly oil a grill rack or broiler-pan rack. Preheat the grill or broiler.

🌿 Meanwhile, in a large saucepan, bring 1½ quarts salted water to a boil over high heat. Add the potatoes and cook for 15 minutes, or until tender when pierced with a knife. Drain well. Place the half-and-half or milk, butter, wasabi paste, and salt in the same saucepan and heat over medium heat to melt the butter. Stir to combine completely. Remove from the heat.

🌿 Add the potatoes to the saucepan and with a potato masher, mash until of desired consistency. Stir in the edamame.

🌿 Grill or broil the salmon for 5 minutes, or until the fish is opaque.

🌿 Evenly divide the potatoes among 4 serving dishes and place in a mound in the center of the dish. Top each with a piece of salmon.

Note: For a less pungent dish, reduce the wasabi paste to 1 teaspoon.

Makes 4 servings

SEA BASS EN PAPILLOTE

Prep time: 5 minutes • Cook time: 15 minutes

PHOTOGRAPH ON PAGE 65

4 teaspoons extra-virgin olive oil

4 teaspoons balsamic vinegar

½ teaspoon salt

½ teaspoon freshly ground black pepper

1 cup shelled edamame

½ cup sun-dried tomatoes in herbed oil, cut into thin strips

½ cup shiitake or button mushrooms, sliced

1½ pounds sea bass, snapper, or cod, skinned and cut into 4 pieces

Preheat the oven to 425°F. Cut 4 pieces, 12" each, of parchment paper or heavy-duty foil.

In a small bowl, combine the oil, vinegar, salt, and pepper. Evenly divide the edamame, tomatoes, and mushrooms and place in the center of each piece of parchment or foil. Top each with a piece of fish. Evenly divide the oil mixture and drizzle over the fish. Bring the parchment or foil over the fish and roll to seal. Seal the sides of each to form a packet.

Place the packets on a large baking sheet and cook for 15 minutes, or until the fish is opaque.

Makes 4 servings

Edamame

98

CURRIED SCALLOPS

4 tablespoons extra-virgin olive oil

1 large carrot, cut into matchsticks

1 large rib celery, cut into matchsticks

1 red onion, cut into thin strips

1 cup shelled edamame

2 teaspoons curry powder

½ teaspoon salt

1 pound sea scallops

2 large tomatoes, chopped

¼ cup sour cream

🌿 Heat 2 tablespoons of the oil in a large skillet over medium-high heat. Add the carrot, celery, onion, and edamame and cook for 7 minutes, or until tender-crisp. Remove to a serving plate and cover to keep warm.

🌿 On a plate, combine the curry powder and salt. Add the scallops and toss to coat the scallops with the curry mixture.

🌿 Add the remaining 2 tablespoons oil to the same skillet. Heat over medium-high heat. Add the scallops and cook over medium heat, turning occasionally, for 5 minutes, or until lightly browned. Add the tomatoes and bring to a boil. Reduce the heat to low and cook for 2 minutes, or until the scallops are cooked through. Remove from the heat. Let cool for 1 minute. Stir in the sour cream.

🌿 Serve over the vegetables.

Makes 4 servings

CHICKEN POT PIE

¼ cup butter

1 pound boneless, skinless chicken breasts, cut into 1" cubes

2 carrots, chopped

2 ribs celery, chopped

1 large onion, chopped

1 cup shelled edamame

1½ teaspoons dried thyme, crushed

2 tablespoons all-purpose flour

½ teaspoon salt

¼ teaspoon freshly ground black pepper

2 cups half-and-half

½ cup Parmesan or Romano cheese

1 tube (16 ounces) prepared polenta, cut into ½" slices

🌿 Preheat the oven to 425°F. Grease a deep 3-quart baking dish.

🌿 Heat 1 tablespoon of the butter in a large skillet over medium-high heat. Add the chicken and cook, stirring frequently, until browned. Using a slotted spoon, remove to the prepared baking dish. Add 1 tablespoon butter and cook the carrots, celery, onion, edamame, and thyme for 5 minutes, or until tender-crisp. Place in the baking dish with the chicken.

🌿 Melt the remaining 2 tablespoons butter in the same skillet over medium-high heat. Add the flour, salt, and pepper and cook, stirring constantly, for 3 minutes, or until the flour is lightly browned.

🌿 Stir in the half-and-half and cook for 3 minutes, or until thick and bubbling. Stir in ¼ cup of the cheese. Pour into the baking dish with the chicken and vegetables. Place the slices of polenta over the top and sprinkle with the remaining ¼ cup cheese. Bake for 20 minutes, or until hot and bubbling.

Makes 4 servings

SPICED PORK ROAST

1 teaspoon ground cinnamon

1 teaspoon ground ginger

1 teaspoon salt

¼ teaspoon ground allspice

1 pork tenderloin roast, about ¾ pound

2 red bell peppers, chopped

1 small butternut squash, peeled, seeded, and cut into ½" cubes

1 onion, chopped

1½ cups shelled edamame

2 tablespoons extra-virgin olive oil

Preheat the oven to 425°F.

In a small bowl, combine the cinnamon, ginger, ½ teaspoon of the salt, and allspice. Rub over the pork roast. Place the roast in a 13" × 9" pan. Surround the roast with the peppers, squash, onion, and edamame; drizzle with the oil and the remaining ½ teaspoon salt, tossing to coat well. Roast for 15 minutes.

Reduce the oven temperature to 350°F and roast for 30 minutes, or until the pork reaches 155°F on an instant-read thermometer and the juices run clear.

Remove the roast to a cutting board, cover with foil, and let stand for 10 minutes. Slice the pork and serve with the vegetables.

Makes 4 servings

BALSAMIC-GLAZED PORK CHOPS

Prep time: 5 minutes • Cook time: 17 minutes

PHOTOGRAPH ON PAGE 67

4 boneless pork chops, ¾" thick

½ teaspoon salt

½ teaspoon freshly ground black pepper

3 tablespoons butter

2 onions, sliced

1 clove garlic, minced

1 cup shelled edamame

1 teaspoon sugar

2 tablespoons balsamic vinegar

🌿 Season the pork chops with the salt and pepper.

🌿 Melt the butter in a large skillet over medium-high heat. Add the pork chops and cook for 5 minutes, or until browned, turning once. Remove the chops to a serving platter, cover, and keep warm.

🌿 Add the onions, garlic, edamame, and sugar to the skillet and cook for 8 minutes, stirring occasionally, or until the onions are tender. Add the vinegar and cook, stirring for 2 minutes, or until syrupy. Return the chops to the skillet and cook for 2 minutes to heat through.

Makes 4 servings

GRILLED FLANK STEAK
WITH JEWELED SALSA

Steak

2 tablespoons extra-virgin olive oil

1 clove garlic, minced

1 teaspoon ground cumin

1 teaspoon salt

½ teaspoon dried oregano, crushed

1 beef flank steak, about 1½ pounds

Salsa

2 tablespoons fresh lime juice

2 tablespoons extra-virgin olive oil

¼ cup fresh cilantro, chopped

1 clove garlic, minced

½ teaspoon salt

¼ teaspoon freshly ground black pepper

1 large tomato, chopped

1 cup shelled, cooked edamame

1 ear corn, kernels cut from the cob (1 cup)

🌿 *To make the steak:* In a small bowl, combine the oil, garlic, cumin, salt, and oregano. Place the steak on a platter and rub the cumin mixture over both sides of the steak. Let stand at room temperature for 20 minutes.

🌿 Lightly oil a grill rack or broiler-pan rack. Preheat the grill or broiler.

🌿 *To make the salsa:* In a medium bowl, whisk together the lime juice, oil, cilantro, garlic, salt, and pepper. Add the tomato, edamame, and corn and toss to coat well. Set aside.

🌿 Grill or broil the steak for 4 minutes per side, or until a thermometer inserted in the center registers 145°F for medium-rare.

🌿 Place the steak on a cutting board and let stand for 10 minutes. Cut the steak into thin slices and serve with the salsa.

Makes 6 servings

ORANGE BEEF STIR-FRY

Prep time: 5 minutes • Cook time: 20 minutes

PHOTOGRAPH ON PAGE 67

1 cup uncooked rice

1 cup beef broth

¼ cup orange marmalade

3 tablespoons soy sauce

2 tablespoons cornstarch

¼ teaspoon crushed red-pepper flakes

3 tablespoons peanut oil

4 scallions, cut into 1" pieces

1 red bell pepper, cut into 1" pieces

1 cup shelled edamame

1 pound beef top round or sirloin steak, cut into thin strips

✑ Prepare the rice according to package directions.

✑ In a small bowl, whisk together the broth, marmalade, soy sauce, cornstarch, and red-pepper flakes. Set aside.

✑ Heat 1 tablespoon of the oil in a wok or large skillet over high heat. Add the scallions, pepper, and edamame and cook for 4 minutes. Using a slotted spoon, remove to a bowl. Add another tablespoon oil and cook half of the beef for 3 minutes, stirring frequently, until crisp and lightly browned on both sides. Place in the bowl with the vegetables. Repeat with the remaining oil and beef. Remove to the bowl.

✑ Stir the broth mixture in the bowl and add to the wok or skillet. Bring to a boil and cook for 2 minutes, or until thickened. Return the beef and vegetables to the wok or skillet and cook for 1 minute to heat through. Serve over the rice.

Makes 4 servings

Edamame

PICADILLO

1 cup uncooked rice

2 tablespoons extra-virgin olive oil

1 onion, chopped

1 yellow bell pepper, chopped

2 cloves garlic, minced

1 pound ground beef and/or pork

1 can (15 ounces) diced tomatoes, drained

1 cup shelled edamame

½ cup pimiento-stuffed olives, chopped

½ cup raisins

1 tablespoon red wine vinegar

2 tablespoons chili powder

1 teaspoon ground cumin

½ teaspoon salt

Prepare the rice according to package directions.

Meanwhile, heat the oil in a large skillet over medium-high heat. Add the onion and pepper and cook for 5 minutes, or until tender. Add the garlic and meat and cook, stirring to break up the meat, for 5 minutes, or until no longer pink.

Stir in the tomatoes, edamame, olives, raisins, vinegar, chili powder, cumin, and salt. Bring to a boil over medium-high heat. Reduce the heat to medium-low and simmer for 5 minutes, or until slightly thickened.

Serve over the rice.

Makes 4 servings

ROSEMARY LAMB KEBABS ON COUSCOUS

Prep time: 4 hours • Cook time: 7 minutes
PHOTOGRAPH ON PAGE 64

¼ cup + 1 tablespoon extra-virgin olive oil

¼ cup fresh lemon juice

2 cloves garlic, minced

1 tablespoon fresh rosemary, minced

½ teaspoon salt

1 pound lamb shoulder, cut into 2" cubes

1 yellow bell pepper, cut into 1½" pieces

1 small zucchini, cut into 1½" pieces

1 cup cherry tomatoes

1 cup shelled edamame

1½ cups couscous

2 cups vegetable broth

🌿 In a medium bowl, whisk together ¼ cup of the oil, the lemon juice, garlic, rosemary, and salt. Add the lamb and toss to coat well. Cover and marinate in the refrigerator for 4 hours or overnight.

🌿 Lightly oil a grill rack or broiler-pan rack. Preheat the grill or broiler.

🌿 Thread the lamb onto 12 skewers (10" each), alternating with the pepper, zucchini, and tomatoes. Grill or broil for 7 minutes, or until the lamb is pink.

🌿 Meanwhile, heat the remaining 1 tablespoon oil in a medium saucepan over medium-high heat. Add the edamame and couscous and cook for 2 minutes. Add the broth and bring to a boil over high heat. Reduce the heat to low, cover, and simmer for 5 minutes, or until the liquid is absorbed.

🌿 To serve, evenly divide the couscous onto 6 plates. Top each with 2 skewers.

Makes 6 servings

SIDE DISHES

From rice to vegetable dishes,
edamame add color and pizzazz
to these accompaniments

BALSAMIC-GLAZED WINTER VEGETABLES

Prep time: 20 minutes • Cook time: 45 minutes
PHOTOGRAPH ON PAGE 68

2 medium sweet potatoes, peeled and cut into 1¼" cubes

2 large carrots, cut into ½" pieces

2 large parsnips, cut into ½" pieces

2 large turnips, cut into ½" pieces

1 cup shelled edamame

2 cloves garlic, minced

1 tablespoon minced fresh rosemary

3 tablespoons extra-virgin olive oil

¾ teaspoon salt

½ teaspoon freshly ground black pepper

2 tablespoons balsamic vinegar

1 tablespoon honey

Preheat the oven to 450°F.

In a shallow roasting pan, combine the sweet potatoes, carrots, parsnips, turnips, edamame, garlic, rosemary, oil, salt, and pepper. Spread in an even layer and bake for 30 minutes.

Meanwhile, in a small bowl, combine the vinegar and honey. Drizzle over the vegetables and toss to coat. Bake for 15 minutes, or until the vegetables are tender and golden brown.

Makes 6 servings

CURRIED CAULIFLOWER

Prep time: 4 minutes • Cook time: 17 minutes

½ cup apple cider or juice

1 tablespoon honey

2 teaspoons finely chopped fresh ginger

1½ teaspoons curry powder

¼ teaspoon ground cumin

¾ teaspoon salt

1 medium head cauliflower, cut into florets

1 cup shelled edamame

¼ cup sour cream

¼ cup fresh cilantro, chopped

In a large skillet, combine the cider or juice, honey, ginger, curry powder, cumin, and salt. Arrange the cauliflower in a single layer in the skillet and scatter the edamame on top. Bring to a boil over medium heat, cover, and cook for 8 minutes, or just until the cauliflower is tender. Remove the cauliflower and edamame with a slotted spoon to a serving bowl. Cover to keep warm.

Bring the cooking liquid to a boil and cook for 8 minutes, or until reduced to a thick syrup. Stir in the sour cream and cilantro. Cook for 1 minute. Pour over the cauliflower mixture.

Makes 6 servings

ITALIAN STUFFED TOMATOES

8 ripe medium tomatoes (about 2¼ pounds), tops
   cut off

1 cup chicken broth

1 tablespoon extra-virgin olive oil

½ cup Arborio rice

2 large shallots, chopped

1 clove garlic, minced

¼ teaspoon dried thyme, crushed

¾ cup shelled, cooked edamame

½ cup fresh basil, chopped

¼ teaspoon salt

¼ teaspoon freshly ground black pepper

⅓ cup grated Parmesan cheese

🌿 Preheat the oven to 350°F.

🌿 Place a sieve in a medium bowl. Scoop the flesh out of the tomatoes and set in the sieve. Press out the juice from the tomato flesh and reserve for the rice cooking (you should have about ⅔ cup). Place the hollowed tomatoes in an 11" × 7" baking dish.

🌿 Combine the broth and reserved tomato liquid in a 2-cup measure. Microwave at full power for 2 minutes, or until almost boiling.

🌿 Heat the oil in a medium saucepan over medium heat. Stir in the rice, shallots, garlic, and thyme. Cook for 2 minutes, stirring occasionally. Add ½ cup of the broth mixture and cook, stirring occasionally, until the liquid is almost absorbed. Stir in ¼ cup broth mixture. Repeat the cooking process, adding ¼ cup broth at a time until the rice is just cooked through but still has a slight bite to it. (The entire cooking time is about 23 minutes.)

🌿 Remove from the heat and stir in the edamame, basil, salt, pepper, and ¼ cup of the cheese. Spoon the rice mixture into the tomato shells and sprinkle the remaining cheese on top. Bake for 20 minutes, or until lightly browned. Serve hot or at room temperature.

Makes 4 servings

SUCCOTASH WITH OKRA AND EDAMAME

Prep time: 10 minutes • Cook time: 16 minutes

PHOTOGRAPH ON PAGE 69

2 tablespoons extra-virgin olive oil

4 large shallots, chopped

2 ears corn, kernels cut from the cob (or 2 cups frozen corn kernels)

½ teaspoon Italian seasoning

1 cup shelled edamame

1 cup frozen sliced okra, thawed

2 medium tomatoes, chopped

½ teaspoon salt

¼ teaspoon freshly ground black pepper

¼ cup fresh basil, chopped

🌿 Heat the oil in a large skillet over medium-high heat. Add the shallots, corn, and Italian seasoning and cook for 8 minutes, stirring occasionally.

🌿 Stir in the edamame, okra, tomatoes, salt, and pepper. Bring to a simmer and cook for 8 minutes, or until the vegetables are tender. Stir in the basil.

Makes 4 servings

GREEN BEANS AND EDAMAME À LA GRECQUE

Prep time: 15 minutes • Cook time: 15 minutes
PHOTOGRAPH ON PAGE 70

¾ pound green beans, cut into 1½" lengths

1½ cups shelled edamame

2 tablespoons extra-virgin olive oil

1 small red onion, cut into thin strips

1 large clove garlic, minced

1 can (15 ounces) diced tomatoes

1 teaspoon dried oregano

1 teaspoon freshly grated lemon peel

¼ teaspoon sugar

¼ teaspoon freshly ground black pepper

Fill a large skillet halfway with salted water and bring to a boil over high heat. Add the beans, bring to a simmer, and cook for 3 minutes. Stir in the edamame and simmer for 4 minutes, or until the beans and edamame are almost tender. Drain well.

Wipe the skillet dry and heat the oil in the skillet over medium heat. Add the onion and garlic and cook for 3 minutes. Stir in the tomatoes (with juice), oregano, lemon peel, sugar, pepper, and the drained vegetables. Bring to a simmer, cover, and cook for 5 minutes, or until the beans are tender.

Makes 4 servings

CORN AND EDAMAME CUSTARDS

1½ cups whole milk

2 tablespoons all-purpose flour

1 scallion, sliced

2 ears corn, kernels cut from the cob
(or 2 cups frozen corn kernels)

¾ cup shelled, cooked edamame

2 eggs

2 teaspoons sugar

½ teaspoon salt

⅛ teaspoon freshly ground white pepper

1 teaspoon finely chopped fresh tarragon

🍃 Preheat the oven to 325°F. Grease six 6-ounce custard cups. Place the cups in a 13" × 9" baking dish. Fill a large bowl with ice. Add cold water and set aside.

🍃 Process the milk, flour, scallion, 1 cup of the corn, and ⅓ cup of the edamame in a blender until smooth.

🍃 Strain through a sieve into a medium saucepan, pressing the solids to extract all of the liquid. Bring to a simmer over medium heat, whisking constantly, and cook for 1 minute. Remove from the heat and set the pan over the prepared ice water. Whisk occasionally for 15 minutes, or until the mixture is barely warm to the touch.

🍃 Meanwhile, chop the remaining edamame and add to the saucepan. Add the eggs, sugar, salt, pepper, tarragon, and remaining corn, whisking until blended. Evenly divide the mixture into the prepared cups. Add 4 cups simmering water to the pan to come halfway up the sides of the cups.

🍃 Bake for 55 minutes, or until set in the center and a knife inserted comes out clean. Transfer to a rack and let stand for at least 15 minutes.

Makes 6 servings

SWEET SPICED EGGPLANT

    2 tablespoons extra-virgin olive oil
    1 large onion, chopped
    1 medium eggplant, peeled and cut into
      ¾" chunks
    1 can (15 ounces) diced tomatoes
    2 tablespoons honey
    1 tablespoon white wine vinegar
    2 cloves garlic, minced
    1 tablespoon minced fresh ginger
 1½ teaspoons ground cumin
    ¾ teaspoon ground coriander
    ½ teaspoon ground fennel
    ½ teaspoon salt
    1 cup shelled edamame
    ⅓ cup fresh cilantro, chopped

Heat the oil in a large skillet over medium heat. Add the onion and cook for 5 minutes, or until softened. Add the eggplant and cook for 3 minutes. Stir in the tomatoes (with juice), honey, vinegar, garlic, ginger, cumin, coriander, fennel, and salt. Bring to a boil over high heat. Reduce the heat to low, cover, and simmer for 8 minutes.

Stir in the edamame and half of the cilantro. Simmer for 8 minutes, or until the eggplant and edamame are tender. Stir in the remaining cilantro.

Makes 4 servings

SESAME SPINACH AND EDAMAME

Prep time: 10 minutes • Cook time: 15 minutes

1 tablespoon sesame seeds

3 tablespoons toasted sesame oil

1 small red onion, halved and thinly sliced

¾ cup shelled edamame

2 teaspoons minced fresh ginger

¼ teaspoon hot-pepper sauce

¼ cup water

10 ounces fresh spinach, rinsed well and stemmed

½ teaspoon salt

⅛ teaspoon freshly ground black pepper

🌿 Heat a skillet over medium heat for 1 minute. Add the sesame seeds and cook, shaking the pan occasionally for 4 minutes, or until toasted and golden. Set aside on a small plate to cool.

🌿 Heat 2 tablespoons of the oil in the same skillet. Add the onion and cook, stirring occasionally, for 4 minutes. Add the edamame, ginger, hot-pepper sauce, and water. Cover and cook for 3 minutes, or until the liquid is almost evaporated. Increase the heat to high and add the spinach, salt, and pepper. Cook for 4 minutes, stirring down the spinach as it wilts, until tender and the liquid has evaporated.

🌿 Remove from the heat and stir in the remaining 1 tablespoon sesame oil. Place in a serving dish and top with the sesame seeds.

Makes 4 servings

SAUTÉED BABY BOK CHOY AND EDAMAME

Prep time: 15 minutes • Cook time: 11 minutes

1 tablespoon + 1½ teaspoons fresh lemon juice

3 tablespoons water

1 tablespoon honey

2 teaspoons soy sauce

1½ teaspoons grated fresh ginger

¾ teaspoon cornstarch

⅛ teaspoon salt

1 tablespoon extra-virgin olive oil

1 pound baby bok choy, stems and leaves separated and sliced 1" thick

1 red or orange bell pepper, cut into ½" pieces

4 scallions, diagonally sliced

1 cup shelled, cooked edamame

In a small bowl, whisk together the lemon juice, water, honey, soy sauce, ginger, cornstarch, and salt until blended.

Heat the oil in a wok or large nonstick skillet over medium-high heat. Add the bok choy stems and the pepper and cook for 7 minutes. Add the bok choy leaves and the scallions. Cook for 3 minutes, or until the vegetables are tender-crisp. Add the stirred lemon-soy mixture and the edamame. Bring to a simmer, stirring constantly, and cook until thickened, about 1 minute.

Makes 4 servings

CREAMY RISOTTO

Prep time: 10 minutes • Cook time: 35 minutes

PHOTOGRAPH ON PAGE 68

6 cups vegetable broth

½ cup dry white wine

2 tablespoons extra-virgin olive oil

2 shallots, minced

2½ cups Arborio rice

1 cup shelled edamame

1 tablespoon butter

1 cup freshly grated Romano cheese

🌿 In a medium saucepan, combine the broth and wine. Bring to a boil over high heat. Reduce the heat to low, cover, and simmer.

🌿 Heat the oil in another medium saucepan over medium-high heat. Add the shallots and cook for 2 minutes. Add the rice and cook, stirring frequently, for 3 minutes. Add about ½ cup of the broth, reduce the heat to medium-low, and cook, stirring constantly, until the liquid is absorbed. Continue adding the broth, ½ cup at a time, stirring constantly after each addition until the liquid is absorbed and the rice is tender yet firm to the bite (about 30 minutes), adding the edamame with the last addition of broth.

🌿 Stir in the butter and cheese.

Makes 6 servings

TOASTED BARLEY
AND EDAMAME PILAF

½ cup quick-cooking barley

1 cup chicken broth

4 shallots, minced

¼ teaspoon salt

¼ teaspoon freshly ground black pepper

1 cup shelled edamame

1 tablespoon + 1½ teaspoons finely chopped fresh sage

2 tablespoons extra-virgin olive oil

8 ounces sliced button mushrooms

2 small portobello mushrooms (6 ounces), thinly sliced and cut into 1" pieces

2 tablespoons dry sherry

🌿 Heat a large skillet over medium heat. Add the barley and toast, shaking the pan and stirring frequently, for 5 minutes, or until the barley turns brown and has a nutty aroma. (Watch the pan and shake more frequently during the last 2 minutes of the cooking.) Place on a small plate and set aside.

🌿 In a small saucepan, bring the broth, shallots, salt, and pepper to a simmer. Add the barley, return to a simmer, and cook, covered, for 5 minutes. Stir in the edamame, cover, and simmer for 5 minutes longer, or until the barley is tender. Remove from the heat, stir in the sage, and set aside.

🌿 Meanwhile, heat the oil in the skillet set over high heat. Add the mushrooms and cook for 5 minutes, stirring after 2 minutes of cooking. Cook until all of the liquid has evaporated and the mushrooms are golden. Add the sherry and cook for 1 minute, or until the sherry has evaporated. Stir in the barley mixture and cook for 1 minute, or until heated through.

Makes 4 servings

Index

Boldfaced page references indicate photographs.

126

Thai Vegetable Bowl, 88
Vegetable Handrolls, 30–31, **56**
Asparagus
Roasted Asparagus Salad, 34, **58**
Vegetable Handrolls, 30–31, **56**
Avocados
Cobb Salad with Edamame, 46
Guacamole, 16–17

B

Balsamic-Glazed Pork Chops, **67**, 103
Balsamic-Glazed Winter Vegetables,
68, 112
Barley
Hearty Vegetable Beef Soup, **61**,
74–75
Toasted Barley and Edamame Pilaf,
124–25
Basil
Italian Stuffed Tomatoes, 114–15
Lebanese Pita Salad, 43
Pasta Primavera, 90–91
Penne with Edamame and Goat
Cheese Sauce, **63**, 89
Simple Bruschetta, 24–25, **57**
Soupe au Pistou, 82–83
Succotash with Okra and Edamame,
69, 116
Tabbouleh Salad with Mint and
Basil, 42
Beans
Green Beans and Edamame à la
Grecque, **70**, 117
Soupe au Pistou, 82–83
Vegetable Chili, 86
Beef
Grilled Flank Steak with Jeweled
Salsa, **66**, 104–5
Hearty Vegetable Beef Soup, **61**,
74–75
Orange Beef Stir-Fry, **67**, 106
Picadillo, 107
Bell peppers
Broccoli and Cauliflower Salad, 35
Corn and Edamame Chowder, 71
Lebanese Pita Salad, 43
Miso Edamame Soup, 72–73
Orange Beef Stir-Fry, **67**, 106

Pasta Primavera, 90–91
Pasta with Swiss Chard and Ricotta,
92–93
Picadillo, 107
Roasted Asparagus Salad, 34, **58**
Rosemary Lamb Kebabs on
Couscous, **64**, 108–9
Sautéed Baby Bok Choy and
Edamame, 122
Spiced Pork Roast, 102
Vegetable Chili, 86
Vegetable Lasagna, 94–95
Warm Scallop and Edamame Salad,
47, **60**
Bok choy
Sautéed Baby Bok Choy and
Edamame, 122
Breads. *See also* Tortillas
Lebanese Pita Salad, 43
Simple Bruschetta, 24–25, **57**
Broccoli
Broccoli and Cauliflower Salad, 35
Pasta Primavera, 90–91
Broccoli and Cauliflower Salad, 35
Bruschetta
Simple Bruschetta, 24–25, **57**
Bulgur wheat
Tabbouleh Salad with Mint and
Basil, 42
Burgers
Veggie Burgers, **63**, 87

C

Cabbage
Sautéed Baby Bok Choy and
Edamame, 122
Tuscan Minestrone with Orzo, 52–53
Carrots
Balsamic-Glazed Winter Vegetables,
68, 112
Chicken Pot Pie, 100–101
Curried Scallops, 99
Hearty Vegetable Beef Soup, **61**,
74–75
Pasta Primavera, 90–91
Summer Garden Vegetable Soup,
50–51, **62**
Thai Seafood Soup, **61**, 78–79

Lettuce
  Cobb Salad with Edamame, 46
  Frisée Salad with Pancetta and
    Seared Shallots, 38, **59**
  Grilled Tomatoes with Edamame and
    Goat Cheese, 36–37
  Roasted Asparagus Salad, 34, **58**
  Warm Scallop and Edamame Salad,
    47, **60**

M
Main dishes (meat)
  Balsamic-Glazed Pork Chops, **67**,
    103
  Grilled Flank Steak with Jeweled
    Salsa, **66**, 104–5
  Orange Beef Stir-Fry, **67**, 106
  Picadillo, 107
  Rosemary Lamb Kebabs on
    Couscous, **64**, 108–9
  Spiced Pork Roast, 102
Main dishes (meatless)
  Pasta Primavera, 90–91
  Pasta with Swiss Chard and Ricotta,
    92–93
  Penne with Edamame and Goat
    Cheese Sauce, **63**, 89
  Thai Vegetable Bowl, 88
  Vegetable Chili, 86
  Vegetable Lasagna, 94–95
  Veggie Burgers, **63**, 87
Main dishes (poultry)
  Chicken Pot Pie, 100–101
  Cobb Salad with Edamame, 46
Main dishes (seafood)
  Asian Salmon and Wasabi Mashed
    Potatoes, **65**, 96–97
  Curried Scallops, 99
  Sea Bass en Papillote, **65**, 98
  Warm Scallop and Edamame Salad,
    47, **60**
Meat. *See* Beef; Lamb; Pork
Mediterranean-style dishes
  Green Beans and Edamame à la
    Grecque, **70**, 117
  Lebanese Pita Salad, 43
  Rosemary Lamb Kebabs on
    Couscous, **64**, 108–9

Soupe au Pistou, 82–83
Tabbouleh Salad with Mint and
  Basil, 42
Mint
  Lebanese Pita Salad, 43
  Tabbouleh Salad with Mint and
    Basil, 42
Miso
  Broccoli and Cauliflower Salad, 35
  Miso Edamame Soup, 72–73
Miso Edamame Soup, 72–73
Mushrooms
  Hearty Vegetable Beef Soup, **61**,
    74–75
  Miso Edamame Soup, 72–73
  Roasted Portobello and Shallot
    Salad, 40–41
  Savory Mushroom Tart, 22–23, **55**
  Sea Bass en Papillote, **65**, 98
  Thai Seafood Soup, **61**, 78–79
  Toasted Barley and Edamame Pilaf,
    124–25
Mussels
  Thai Seafood Soup, **61**, 78–79
Mustardy Potato Salad, 39

O
Okra
  Succotash with Okra and Edamame,
    69, 116
Orange Beef Stir-Fry, **67**, 106
Orzo
  Tuscan Minestrone with Orzo, 52–53

P
Pancetta
  Frisée Salad with Pancetta and
    Seared Shallots, 38, **59**
Pasta
  Pasta Primavera, 90–91
  Pasta with Swiss Chard and Ricotta,
    92–93
  Penne with Edamame and Goat
    Cheese Sauce, **63**, 89
  Rosemary Lamb Kebabs on
    Couscous, **64**, 108–9
  Sesame-Ginger Couscous Salad,
    44–45, **59**

I n d e x

Soupe au Pistou, 82–83
Thai Vegetable Bowl, 88
Tuscan Minestrone with Orzo, 52–53
Vegetable Lasagna, 94–95
Pasta Primavera, 90–91
Pasta with Swiss Chard and Ricotta,
92–93
Penne with Edamame and Goat Cheese
Sauce, **63**, 89
Peppers. *See* Bell peppers; Chile
peppers
Picadillo, 107
Pies
Chicken Pot Pie, 100–101
Savory Mushroom Tart, 22–23, **55**
Pork
Balsamic-Glazed Pork Chops, **67**, 103
Frisée Salad with Pancetta and
Seared Shallots, 38, **59**
Picadillo, 107
Spiced Pork Roast, 102
Potatoes
Asian Salmon and Wasabi Mashed
Potatoes, **65**, 96–97
Balsamic-Glazed Winter Vegetables,
68, 112
Chicken Quesadillas, 18–19
Corn and Edamame Chowder, 71
Curried Croquettes, 26–27, **56**
Mustardy Potato Salad, 39
Soupe au Pistou, 82–83
Tuscan Minestrone with Orzo, 52–53
Poultry. *See* Chicken; Turkey

Q
Quesadillas
Chicken Quesadillas, 18–19

R
Rice
Creamy Risotto, **68**, 123
Italian Stuffed Tomatoes, 114–15
Orange Beef Stir-Fry, **67**, 106
Picadillo, 107
Vegetable Chili, 86
Vegetable Handrolls, 30–31, **56**
Risotto
Creamy Risotto, **68**, 123

Roasted Asparagus Salad, 34, **58**
Roasted Edamame, 13, **57**
Roasted Portobello and Shallot Salad,
40–41
Rosemary
Balsamic-Glazed Winter Vegetables,
68, 112
Rosemary Lamb Kebabs on
Couscous, **64**, 108–9
Zesty Garlic Dip, 15
Rosemary Lamb Kebabs on Couscous,
64, 108–9

S
Salads (main dish)
Cobb Salad with Edamame, 46
Warm Scallop and Edamame Salad,
47, **60**
Salads (side dish)
Broccoli and Cauliflower Salad, 35
Frisée Salad with Pancetta and
Seared Shallots, 38, **59**
Grilled Tomatoes with Edamame and
Goat Cheese, 36–37
Lebanese Pita Salad, 43
Mustardy Potato Salad, 39
Roasted Asparagus Salad, 34, **58**
Roasted Portobello and Shallot
Salad, 40–41
Sesame-Ginger Couscous Salad,
44–45, **59**
Tabbouleh Salad with Mint and
Basil, 42
Salmon
Asian Salmon and Wasabi Mashed
Potatoes, **65**, 96–97
Salsa
Edamame Salsa, 14
Grilled Flank Steak with Jeweled
Salsa, **66**, 104–5
Salted Edamame, 12
Sautéed Baby Bok Choy and Edamame,
122
Savory Mushroom Tart, 22–23, **55**
Scallops
Curried Scallops, 99
Warm Scallop and Edamame Salad,
47, **60**

Index
131

I n d e x

Conversion Chart

These equivalents have been slightly rounded to make measuring easier.

Volume Measurements

U.S.	Imperial	Metric
¼ tsp	–	1 ml
½ tsp	–	2 ml
1 tsp	–	5 ml
1 Tbsp	–	15 ml
2 Tbsp (1 oz)	1 fl oz	30 ml
¼ cup (2 oz)	2 fl oz	60 ml
⅓ cup (3 oz)	3 fl oz	80 ml
½ cup (4 oz)	4 fl oz	120 ml
⅔ cup (5 oz)	5 fl oz	160 ml
¾ cup (6 oz)	6 fl oz	180 ml
1 cup (8 oz)	8 fl oz	240 ml

Weight Measurements

U.S.	Metric
1 oz	30 g
2 oz	60 g
4 oz (¼ lb)	115 g
5 oz (⅓ lb)	145 g
6 oz	170 g
7 oz	200 g
8 oz (½ lb)	230 g
10 oz	285 g
12 oz (¾ lb)	340 g
14 oz	400 g
16 oz (1 lb)	455 g
2.2 lb	1 kg

Length Measurements

U.S.	Metric
¼"	0.6 cm
½"	1.25 cm
1"	2.5 cm
2"	5 cm
4"	11 cm
6"	15 cm
8"	20 cm
10"	25 cm
12" (1')	30 cm

Pan Sizes

U.S.	Metric
8" cake pan	20 × 4 cm sandwich or cake tin
9" cake pan	23 × 3.5 cm sandwich or cake tin
11" × 7" baking pan	28 × 18 cm baking tin
13" × 9" baking pan	32.5 × 23 cm baking tin
15" × 10" baking pan	38 × 25.5 cm baking tin (Swiss roll tin)
1½ qt baking dish	1.5 liter baking dish
2 qt baking dish	2 liter baking dish
2 qt rectangular baking dish	30 × 19 cm baking dish
9" pie plate	22 × 4 or 23 × 4 cm pie plate
7" or 8" springform pan	18 or 20 cm springform or loose-bottom cake tin
9" × 5" loaf pan	23 × 13 cm or 2 lb narrow loaf tin or pâté tin

Temperatures

Fahrenheit	Centigrade	Gas
140°	60°	–
160°	70°	–
180°	80°	–
225°	105°	¼
250°	120°	½
275°	135°	1
300°	150°	2
325°	160°	3
350°	180°	4
375°	190°	5
400°	200°	6
425°	220°	7
450°	230°	8
475°	245°	9
500°	260°	–